EAST GERMAN POETRY

EAST GERMAN POETRY

An Anthology

edited by Michael Hamburger

E. P. Dutton & Co., Inc. | New York | 1973

English translations and Introduction
Copyright © 1973 by Michael Hamburger, Christopher Middleton,
Christopher Levenson, Ruth and Matthew Mead,
Gordon and Gisela Brotherston

All rights reserved. Printed in Great Britain.

831
H

First Edition

No part of this publication may be reproduced or
transmitted in any form or by any means, electronic
or mechanical, including photocopy, recording, or any
information storage and retrieval system now known
or to be invented, without permission in writing
from the publisher, except by a reviewer who wishes
to quote brief passages in connection with a review
for inclusion in a magazine, newspaper or broadcast.

Published simultaneously in Canada
by Clarke, Irwin & Company Limited, Toronto and Vancouver

Library of Congress Catalog Card Number: 73-158584
SBN 0-525-09668-X—cloth   0-525-03310-6—paper

The editor and translators wish to thank the following German publishers
for the right to reproduce and translate the poems in this book: Biederstein
Verlag, Munich: Kurt Bartsch, poems from the anthology *Aussichten*,
© 1966. S. Fischer Verlag, Frankfurt am Main: Peter Huchel, *Chausseen
Chausseen* © 1963; Reiner Kunze, *Zimmerlautstärke* © 1972. Carl Hanser
Verlag, Munich: Günter Kunert, *Erinnerung an einen Planeten* © 1963;
Tagträume © 1964; *Verkündigung des Wetters* © 1966; *Warnung vor Spiegeln*
© 1970. Rowohlt Verlag, Hamburg: Reiner Kunze, *Sensible Wege* ©
1969; Karl Mickel, *Vita Nova Mea* © 1967. Suhrkamp Verlag, Frankfurt
am Main: Bertolt Brecht, *Gedichte 3*, Gesammelte Werke, Band 10 © 1967;
Volker Braun, *Vorläufiges* © 1966; *Wir und nicht Sie* © 1970. Verlag
Klaus Wagenbach, West Berlin: Wolf Biermann, *Mit Marx- und
Engelszungen* © 1968; Johannes Bobrowski, *Wetterzeichen* © 1966;
Tintenfisch 4, © 1971.

The editor's thanks are also due to the New York State Council for the
Arts, under whose auspices the anthology was begun.

CONTENTS

BERTOLT BRECHT *Translated by Michael Hamburger*

PETER HUCHEL *Translated by Michael Hamburger, Christopher Levenson, and Christopher Middleton*

JOHANNES BOBROWSKI *Translated by Ruth and Matthew Mead*

GÜNTER KUNERT *Translated by Michael Hamburger, Christopher Levenson, and Christopher Middleton*

Introduction

THE political division of Germany into two separate republics makes it necessary to begin by saying what kind of anthology I have put together. It is not a representative anthology in terms of the political division, since that would have called for the inclusion of the sort of verse most in favor with the ideological directors of the régime—exhortatory, self-congratulating pep-verse, antiquated even by the standards of the eighteen-nineties and subliterary in its complete subordination of the medium to the message. Sociologists interested in the officially fostered and celebrated dispensers of versified doctrine are referred to the later work of the former Expressionist poet Johannes R. Becher, author of the Republic's national anthem and Minister of Culture from 1954 until his death in 1958.

The poets included here are those of interest to readers of poetry, as distinct from students of propaganda, outside the German Democratic Republic; and they are of interest to readers of poetry because their commitment is that of true poets anywhere, at any time, to the truth of their own perceptions, feelings, and convictions. Needless to say, their perceptions, feelings, and convictions may differ from those of poets living in other kinds of societies, under other kinds of government; but not so much as to be either incomprehensible or irrelevant on the other side of the Wall. The German texts of most of the poems have been published and read in West Germany. Some of them, like the poems of Peter Huchel and Wolf Biermann, have been published only in West Germany, because East German publication was prohibited.

Yet all these poets chose to live in East Germany, even if the politico-cultural bureaucrats have done their best to make them regret their choice, and all of them chose to stay there when, not so many years ago, they were still free to get out. All of them, beginning with Brecht, have been preoccupied with moral and social problems to a degree rare among non-communist poets; and that is another reason why their work is, or should be, of special interest to American and British readers with no direct experience of an almost totally collectivized society.

Translation acted as an additional filter. It excluded some of the more deliberately public of Brecht's later poems, as well as the work of living poets, such as Stefan Hermlin and Erich Arendt, who would have been included if their diction and verse forms had not proved too remote from the practice of their English-writing contemporaries. Of the younger poets, Karl Mickel would have been more generously represented but for a baroque element in his manner that resisted translation; and Peter Gosse's work proved refractory for related reasons.

It is the more laconic of Brecht's later poems that were of seminal importance to almost all the younger poets whose work is presented here. Peter Huchel and Johannes Bobrowski are the outstanding exceptions, since their vision is of a different order. Huchel's is apocalyptic and elegiac where Brecht—even in so-called elegies which are close to epigram—was coolly and dryly matter-of-fact, or tried to be. Bobrowski's plain words served to create mystery, by means of a syntactic and metrical architecture that made inimitable use of empty spaces. Both these excellent poets have been greatly appreciated in West Germany; but Brecht, again, was the main link between the younger poets of the two nations, because he succeeded better than any other poet of his generation in making social and political awareness the very precondition of writing, while remaining a dialectician even in poetry, getting to grips with real tensions between individual and collective needs—a precedent for the West German poet Hans Magnus Enzensberger as much as for Volker Braun.

The minimal poem evolved by Brecht—minimal not only in length but in economy of gesture, bareness, and ordinariness of diction, avoidance of trope and ornament, reduction of the poetic persona to what is functional or generally human—is a recurrent mode among younger East German poets, from Kunert and Kahlau to Bartsch and Kunze. Like Brecht before them, but more disturbingly, these poets are beset by doubts as to whether the writing of poetry can be useful or meaningful in a social order that has done away with poetry's earlier use as a luxury product for the privileged, leisured, and well-educated.

It is worth noting that the end of poetry was predicted in the early stages of the Industrial Revolution, as by Thomas Love Peacock in 1820; or by Carlyle in 1829, who wrote that virtue was "no longer a worship of the Beautiful and Good; but a calculation of the Profitable." Over the next century or so poetry defended itself by proclaiming its autonomy. Although even Brecht granted that "art is an autonomous realm" (1940), as a Marxist he had to distinguish this autonomy from the autarchy claimed by "bourgeois" poets. His minimal poetry was the outcome of a long process of confrontation and adjustment; it was what was left over after poetry had "washed its language", as he put it, and stripped itself of all dispensable finery.

Younger poets writing after 1945 became obsessed with the indecency of writing poetry at all—lived poetry, as distinct from versified propaganda—because to claim attention for anything personal and individual was felt to be presumptuous. To many poets represented here, as to Tadeusz Różewicz in Poland, even the minimal poem tended to seem too much. Like Różewicz, Reiner Kunze not only defines the superfluous poem and the superfluous poet but enacts the very compulsion of poems to shrink almost to the point of disappearance, in a poem called "Apology". Yet the same poet is a fearless and unapologetic critic of bureaucracy and censorship, less reckless but no less outspoken than Wolf Biermann, whom he has generously defended.

Another young East German poet, Peter Gosse, takes stock in a new year poem as follows:

> Three years, two pounds of verse,
> While my country drudges and sweats.

A similar confrontation with "the Profitable", in terms of the Marxist stress on productive labor—which is becoming less and less distinguishable from the capitalist stress on productive labor—occurs in Kurt Bartsch's poem called "Poetry"; and what Volker Braun says about the "negative poets" of his time springs from the same discomfort.

Yet Volker Braun, Wolf Biermann, and Sarah Kirsch are three poets who have gone beyond the minimal poem, reasserting the value of individuality either explicitly, as Biermann does in his "All-in Tirade",* or implicitly, by a more pronounced idiosyncrasy of diction and imagery. Günter Kunert's development in the sixties also shows a growing readiness to draw on personal

---

* *Rücksichtslose Schimpferei.* My translation of this poem, and of other poems from Biermann's first collection, had to be taken out of the anthology because permission was refused by the American publisher of Eric Bentley's translation of that book.

experience and a gradual liberation from the Brechtian didacticism of his earlier work.

Yet even Biermann's invective should be understood dialectically. His insistence on his own truth is qualified by the words, "liar that I am", that is, by his awareness of the individual's fallibility; and the self asserted in his poems is not the highly differentiated sensibility of individualistic confessional poetry but an "I" so basically human as to be anyone's—a crucial tribute to the Marxist collective against whose busybodies this very poem inveighs. Biermann, after all, left West Germany in order to live in the other Germany which has outlawed him (as Kunze mentions in his defence).

Even Johannes Bobrowski, who was a Christian as well as a Socialist, could not accommodate bourgeois individualism in his poetry. His poem "Absage" ("Forgoing"), one of the very few in which he permitted himself any reference to an "I" that could be identified with his own person, shifts from the Old Prussians (or Pruzzians, a Slav people exterminated in the Middle Ages by the Order of the Teutonic Knights) to this conclusion:

> There
> I was. In an age long past.
> Nothing new has ever begun. I am a man,
> one flesh with his wife,
> who raises his children
> for an age without fear.

In a very different way from Brecht, Bobrowski also reduced his self to a function, a function more traditionally poetic in the greater scope granted to imagination, though to imagination in the service of conscience. Bobrowski and Huchel understood their function largely as a bearing witness not only to the events of the age but also to archetypal and recurrent truths which must be grasped through vision rather than observed, evoked rather than described. Yet both found it as necessary to get rid of the "egotistical sublime" as the practitioners of minimal poetry.

The relation between individual and collective values, then, is a constantly powerful tension in the best East German poetry. The freedoms which these poets demand are freedoms for everyone, not for themselves; and they have had ample opportunity to learn that to fight repressive stupidity is so difficult a business that it needs all one's powers of discrimination; that revolutions tend to devour not only their children but their fathers and grandfathers, while preserving them in effigy to prevent indigestion; and that the better the poetry, the less likely its revolutionary potential is to become widely effective. These are humbling lessons; and the dominant mood of the poems that follow is not cheerful. (Cheerfulness can be left to the official pep purveyors, who are lavishly rewarded for unflagging optimism.) It is only in the teeth of experience that the "principle of hope"—as a former East German, the philosopher Ernst Bloch, calls the utopian spirit of primitive communism—breaks through again and again.

Bobrowski's words,

> Nothing new has ever begun

may seem strange in a poem by an East German and professed Socialist. Huchel and Bobrowski, though, are not alone in their concern with the remote and recent past, as in a very positive engagement with poetic predecessors of past centuries. One reason is that when West German poets eagerly took up the modernism that had been proscribed under Nazism as "degenerate art", Marxist aesthetics had as little patience with the "tradition of the new"—with Dadaism, imagism, surrealism or German expressionism—as the cultural dictators of Nazism. Johannes R. Becher's purging of his modernist manner—a "language washing" which in his case left little but timeless banality—is a typical instance. Only Brecht succeeded in working out a new aesthetic that was also a Marxist aesthetic. That is why he could help the East German poets after him. Yet Brecht too was a tireless adapter of the most various models, ranging from China and Japan to ancient Greece and Rome, from Villon to Shakespeare, Shelley, Kipling, cabaret songs, and jazz lyrics.

Where this use of past conventions and models was positive, it was also discriminating and dialectical. Where it was passively imitative, its results were stultifying and deadening. In many obvious ways East German institutions, including its institutional literature, are extraordinarily old-fashioned. Merely to cross from West Berlin to certain residential suburbs of East Berlin, not to mention its partly reconstructed administrative centre, is to feel that one is going back in time by something like half a century—much the same feeling as one gets from reading representative anthologies of East German verse, except that there the jump is an even longer one. Little details in some of the poems translated for this unrepresentative anthology—like the tablecloth in Kurt Bartsch's "Breakfast"—remind one of what is patriarchal and bourgeois in East German society, as compared with the growing informality of Western ways.

The desire to get to know those ways, to travel in the second and third worlds, is strong among the younger poets and grows stronger the more it is thwarted. (Reiner Kunze's variations on postage stamps and the mail service could not have been written by a poet free to travel where he likes and can afford to go.) Keeping its citizens cooped up is one of the most cruelly and stupidly repressive measures of the East German government, a symptom of the fear of external realities that springs from its moral weakness, its bad conscience; and the bad conscience springs from its repressiveness—a vicious circle that can lead to nothing but reciprocal ill-feeling and mistrust. The same fear that any interest in the non-communist world must be subversively anti-communist led to the shameful treatment that Peter Huchel suffered until he was allowed to leave the country in 1971; and to Biermann's expulsion from the Communist party.

That the poets included here are innovators, within the limits set by their social conscience, not within the limits prescribed by the dogmatists of "social realism", is as much to their credit as their courageous insistence that no government made up of men and women has a moral right to treat other men and women as self-righteous Victorian parents treated their "naughty children"; but this brings us back to the rigidities and hypocrisies of a régime that has carried out economic reforms to the exclusion of all other kinds, such as the psychological, and to the fear of psychological reforms inherent in the system itself. Poetry alone will not lead to a general change of heart; but as long as poets are true to their experience they cannot help upholding a number of basic freedoms, one of which is the freedom to change, to grow, to develop. In that way, if in no other, poetry remains a source of innovation, disturbing enough to those who fear it to be suppressed.

About the translation little needs to be said. All the translators seem to have assumed that it was their job to present as close a rendering as possible of each poet's manner of writing. Whatever the advantages of free imitation for other kinds of verse, poetry as austere as most of this translated here quite naturally calls for a corresponding austerity on the translator's part; a comparable bareness and spareness, which reduce his choice to one of the right word in the right place.

Where the original text is less austere and more playful—like Kunze's song about Biermann—faithfulness not only permits but demands a greater measure of independence. In fact the poem would have been untranslatable if its central conceit, the play on Biermann's name, had had no near-counterpart in the other language (and "Biermann" in German means the man who loads and delivers beer, whereas "beerman" in English does so only by analogy with "milkman" or "postman"). As it was, this translation could only be a relatively free one, since meter and rhyme (of sorts) are more essential to the poem than the literal sense.

Adaptation, transposition, invention, then, are simply part of faithfulness in the rendering of poems, though it is the character of any one poem that suggests how much of these is required. In translating Huchel's poems, too, I took a few small liberties with the sense, toning down epithets whose exact counterparts no longer pull their weight in English poetry. (The, literally, "sublime" brightness of "Behind the Brick Kilns" became merely "noble".)

All the translators who contributed to this anthology must have felt that to use the originals as pretexts for original composition would have offended against the integrity of the poets. That integrity is hard-earned. In America and Britain poets may be tempted by fame or commercial success into becoming showmen, dispensers of easy thrills. If they resist that temptation they have nothing worse to contend with than relative neglect. Biermann is a performing poet with the same temptations and as much fame as he could want in both Germanys; but he cannot retire into private life, with a small circle of readers instead of a mass audience. He must either knuckle under, "swim into the net of self-criticism", as he says—and "self-criticism" is a Communist euphemism for an abject confession of trumped-up guilt—so as to turn into one of the "good boys" of the régime, or else have no readers, no audience at all in his own country. Not to give in under those circumstances takes more than a paring down of one's vanity and greed.

I notice that I have said more about the preconditions of poetry in East Germany than about the quality of the poems translated. In spite of the predominance of minimal poetry, the work included here ranges widely enough—from epigram to prose poem, pure lyric, variation form, and ballad; from expansive talking rhythms to the laconically cryptic; from extreme literalism to the imagistically condensed. Since the translations keep close to the structure of the original poems there was no need to advertise or analyze each poet's way of writing, which will either come through in the English versions or enable readers with some German to cope with the original texts. Nor have I provided the usual biographical notes about each poet, because they rarely add anything worth knowing to the poems themselves, especially where the cult of personality has been as thoroughly abolished as by these poets. All of them are human. All of them want human life—and non-human life—to continue on this planet, "the best that we have".

London, January, 1970   MICHAEL HAMBURGER

Bertolt Brecht
(1898–1956)

Ein neues Haus

Zurückgekehrt nach fünfzehnjährigem Exil
Bin ich eingezogen in ein schönes Haus.
Meine No-Masken und mein Rollbild, den Zweifler zeigend
Habe ich aufgehängt hier. Fahrend durch die Trümmer
Werde ich tagtäglich an die Privilegien erinnert
Die mir dies Haus verschafften. Ich hoffe
Es macht mich nicht geduldig mit den Löchern
In denen so viele Tausende sitzen. Immer noch
Liegt auf dem Schrank mit den Manuskripten
Mein Koffer.

Die Freunde

Mich, den Stückschreiber
Hat der Krieg getrennt von meinem Freund, dem Bühnenbauer.
Die Städte, in denen wir arbeiteten, sind nicht mehr.
Wenn ich durch die Städte gehe, die noch sind
Sage ich mitunter: dieses blaue Stück Wäsche dort
Hätte mein Freund besser plaziert.

Als unsere Städte in Schutt lagen

Als unsere Städte in Schutt lagen
Verwüstet durch den Krieg des Schlächters
Haben wir begonnen, sie wieder aufzubauen
In der Kälte, im Hunger, in der Schwäche.

Die Eisenkärren mit dem Schutt
Zogen wir selber, wie in grauer Vorzeit.
Mit den nackten Händen gruben wir Ziegel aus
Um unsre Kinder nicht in fremde Fron zu verkaufen.

A New House

Back in my country after fifteen years of exile
I have moved into a fine house.
Here I've hung my No masks and picture scroll
Representing the Doubter. As I drive through the ruins
Daily I am reminded of the privileges
That got me this house. I hope
It will not make me patient with the holes
In which so many thousands huddle. Even now
On top of the cupboard containing my manuscripts
My suitcase lies.

The Friends

The war separated
Me, the writer of plays, from my friend the stage designer.
The cities where we worked are no longer there.
When I walk through the cities that are still there
At times I say: that blue piece of washing there,
My friend would have placed it better.

When Our Cities Lay in Ruins

When our cities lay in ruins
Destroyed in the war which the Butcher made
We began to build them up again
In the cold, in our hunger, in our feebleness.

We ourselves pulled the trolleys
Of rubble, as in the gray past.
With our bare hands we dug up the bricks
So as not to sell our children into alien bondage.

Dann machten wir für diese unsere Kinder
In den Schulen Platz und säuberten die Schulen
Und reinigten das Wissen der Jahrhunderte
Vom alten Schmutz, dass es gut für sie sei.

Die Meister kaufen billig ein

Die Bühnenbilder und Kostüme des grossen Neher
Sind gemacht aus billigen Stoffen:
Aus Holz, Rupfen und Farbe
Macht er die baskische Fischerhütte
Und das cäsarische Rom.

So macht meine Freundin aus einem Lächeln
Das sie auf dem Fischmarkt für nichts kriegt
Und das sie wegschenkt wie Fischschuppen
Wenn sie will, ein Ereignis
Das Laotse korrumpiert hätte.

Buckower Elegien

                    Ginge da ein Wind
                    Könnte ich ein Segel stellen.
                    Wäre da kein Segel
                    Machte ich eines aus Stecken und Plane.

I
DER RADWECHSEL

Ich sitze am Strassenrand
Der Fahrer wechselt das Rad.
Ich bin nicht gern, wo ich herkomme.
Ich bin nicht gern, wo ich hinfahre.
Warum sehe ich den Radwechsel
Mit Ungeduld?

Then for those children of ours we made room
In the schools and cleaned the schools
And cleansed their knowledge of the centuries
Of old dirt, to make it fit for children.

Those Who Know Best Buy Cheaply

The décors and costumes of the great Neher
Are made of cheap material:
Out of wood, rags and color
He makes the Basque fisherman's hovel
And Caesar's Rome.

So my woman friend out of a smile
Which she gets for nothing in the fish market
And gives away like the scales of fish
When she wants to, makes an event
That would have bribed Lao-tsu.

Buckow Elegies

> If there were a wind blowing
> I could hoist a sail.
> If there were no sail
> I should make one out of sticks and canvas.

I
CHANGING THE WHEEL

I sit on the roadside verge
The driver changes the wheel.
I do not like the place I have come from
I do not like the place I am going to.
Why with impatience do I
Watch him changing the wheel?

II
DER BLUMENGARTEN

Am See, tief zwischen Tann und Silberpappel
Beschirmt von Mauer und Gesträuch ein Garten
So weise angelegt mit monatlichen Blumen
Dass er vom März bis zum Oktober blüht.

Hier, in der Früh, nicht allzu häufig, sitz ich
Und wünsche mir, auch ich mög allezeit
In den verschiedenen Wettern, guten, schlechten
Dies oder jenes Angenehme zeigen.

III
DIE LÖSUNG

Nach den Aufstand des 17. Juni
Liess der Sekretär des Schriftstellerverbands
In der Stalinallee Flugblätter verteilen
Auf denen zu lesen war, dass das Volk
Das Vertrauen der Regierung verscherzt habe
Und es nur durch verdoppelte Arbeit
Zurückerobern könne. Wäre es da
Nicht doch einfacher, die Regierung
Löste das Volk auf und
Wählte ein anderes?

IV
GROSSE ZEIT, VERTAN

Ich habe gewusst, dass Städte gebaut wurden
Ich bin nicht hingefahren.
Das gehört in die Statistik, dachte ich
Nicht in die Geschichte.

Was sind schon Städte, gebaut
Ohne die Weisheit des Volkes?

II
THE FLOWER GARDEN

Down by the lake, in between fir and poplar,
Sheltered by wall and shrubbery, a garden
So wisely planned with plants for every month
That something blooms from March there to October.

There, not too often, in the early morning
I sit and wish I too in every season,
In all the different weathers, good and bad,
May offer this or that to please men's eyes.

III
THE SOLUTION

After the Uprising on June Seventeenth
The Secretary of the Authors' Union
Had leaflets distributed in the Stalinallee
Which said that the people
Had forfeited the Government's confidence
And could only win it back
By redoubled labor. Wouldn't it
Be simpler in that case if the Government
Dissolved the people and
Elected another?

IV
A GREAT AGE, WASTED

I knew very well that cities were being built
I did not go to see them.
That belongs to statistics, I thought,
Not to history.

What do cities amount to, built
Without the people's wisdom?

V

BÖSER MORGEN

Die Silberpappel, eine ortsbekannte Schönheit
Heut eine alte Vettel. Der See
Eine Lache Abwaschwasser, nicht rühren!
Die Fuchsien unter dem Löwenmaul billig und eitel.
Warum?
Heut nacht im Traum sah ich Finger, auf mich deutend
Wie auf einen Aussätzigen. Sie waren zerarbeitet und
Sie waren gebrochen.

Unwissende! schrie ich
Schuldbewusst.

VI

GEWOHNHEITEN, NOCH IMMER

Die Teller werden hart hingestellt
Dass die Suppe überschwappt.
Mit schriller Stimme
Ertönt das Kommando: Zum Essen!

Der preussische Adler
Den Jungen hackt er
Das Futter in die Mäulchen.

VII

HEISSER TAG

Heisser Tag. Auf den Knien die Schreibmappe
Sitze ich im Pavillon. Ein grüner Kahn
Kommt durch die Weide in Sicht. Im Heck
Eine dicke Nonne, dick gekleidet. Vor ihr
Ein älticher Mensch im Schwimmanzug, wahrscheinlich ein
    Priester.
An der Ruderbank, aus vollen Kräften rudernd
Ein Kind. Wie in alten Zeiten! denke ich
Wie in alten Zeiten!

V
A BAD MORNING

The silver poplar, a beauty of local fame
An old hag today. The lake
A puddle of dirty suds—do not touch.
The fuchsias amid the snapdragons cheap and vain.
But why?
Last night in a dream I saw fingers pointing at me
As at a leper. They were stained with work and
They were broken.

Ignorant lot! I screamed
Full of guilt.

VI
HABITS, EVEN NOW

The plates are put down roughly
So that the soup slops over.
In a shrill voice
They command: Come and get it!

That Prussian eagle
Into the fledglings' gullets
He chops food.

VII
HOT DAY

Hot day. The folder propped on my knees,
I sit in the summerhouse. A dinghy painted green
Appears through the willow tree. In the bow
A heavy nun, heavily clothed. In front of her
An elderly man in a bathing suit, most likely a priest.
On the rowing seat, rowing for all he's worth,
A child. Just like old times, I think,
Just like old times!

VIII
DIE WAHRHEIT EINIGT

Freunde, ich wünschte, ihr wüsstet die Wahrheit und sagte sie!
Nicht wie fliehende müde Cäsaren: Morgen kommt Mehl!
So wie Lenin: Morgen abend
Sind wir verloren, wenn nicht . . .
So wie es im Liedlein heisst:
    „Brüder, mit dieser Frage
    Will ich gleich beginnen:
    Hier aus unsrer schweren Lage
    Gibt es kein Entrinnen."
Freunde, ein kräftiges Eingeständnis
Und ein kräftiges WENN NICHT!

IX
DER RAUCH

Das kleine Haus unter Bäumen am See.
Vom Dach steigt Rauch.
Fehlte er
Wie trostlos dann wären
Haus, Bäume und See.

X
EISEN

Im Traum heute Nacht
Sah ich einen grossen Sturm.
Ins Baugerüst griff er
Den Bauschragen riss er
Den eisernen, abwärts.
Doch was da aus Holz war
Bog sich und blieb.

VIII
TRUTH UNITES US

Friends, I wish that you knew the truth and would speak it!
Not like tired Caesars in flight: Tomorrow flour will arrive!
But like Lenin: Tomorrow night
We shall be done for, unless . . .
Just as the little song has it:
   "Brothers, what it's about
   I'll tell you straight away:
   There is no way out
   Of the fix we're in today."
Friends, a sturdy admission
And a sturdy UNLESS.

IX
SMOKE

The little lakeside house under trees.
From the roof rises smoke.
Without it
How dreary would be
House, trees and lake.

X
IRON

In a dream last night
I saw a great gale rage.
It gripped the scaffolding
Tore down the supports
Of solid iron.
But whatever was made of wood
Gave and remained.

XI
TANNEN

In der Frühe
Sind die Tannen kupfern.
So sah ich sie
Vor einem halben Jahrhundert
Vor zwei Weltkriegen
Mit jungen Augen.

XII
DER EINARMIGE IM GEHÖLZ

Schweisstriefend bückt er sich
Nach dem dürren Reisig. Die Stechmücken
Verjagt er durch Kopfschütteln. Zwischen den Knieen
Bündelt er mühsam das Brennholz. Ächzend
Richtet er sich auf, streckt die Hand hoch, zu spüren
Ob es regnet. Die Hand hoch
Der gefürchtete SS-Mann.

XIII
VOR ACHT JAHREN

Da war eine Zeit
Da war alles hier anders.
Die Metzgerfrau weiss es.
Der Postbote hat einen zu aufrechten Gang.
Und was war der Elektriker?

XIV
RUDERN, GESPRÄCHE

Es ist Abend. Vorbei gleiten
Zwei Faltboote, darinnen
Zwei nackte junge Männer: Nebeneinander rudernd
Sprechen sie. Sprechend
Rudern sie nebeneinander.

XI
FIRS

In the early morning
The firs are copper colored.
That's how I saw them
Fifty years ago
Before two world wars
With eyes that were young.

XII
THE ONE-ARMED MAN IN THE SPINNEY

Dripping with sweat he bends down
For brittle sticks. Driving off
The mosquitoes by shaking his head. Between
His knees laboriously bundles the sticks. With groans
Straightens his back, raising his hand to feel
Whether it's raining. His hand raised
The dreaded SS-man.

XIII
EIGHT YEARS AGO

There was a time
When all was different here.
The butcher's wife knows it.
The postman walks with too straight a back.
And what was the electrician?

XIV
PADDLING, TALKING

It's evening. Two canoes
Glide past, inside them
Two naked young men: Paddling abreast
They talk. Talking
They paddle abreast.

XV
BEIM LESEN DES HORAZ

Selbst die Sintflut
Dauerte nicht ewig.
Einmal verrannen
Die schwarzen Gewässer.
Freilich, wie wenige
Dauerten länger!

XVI
LAUTE

Später, im Herbst
Hausen in den Silberpappeln grosse Schwärme von Krähen
Aber den ganzen Sommer durch höre ich
Da die Gegend vogellos ist
Nur Laute von Menschen rührend.
Ich bin's zufrieden.

XVII
BEI DER LEKTÜRE EINES SOWJETISCHEN BUCHES

Die Wolga, lese ich, zu bezwingen
Wird keine leichte Aufgabe sein. Sie wird
Ihre Töchter zu Hilfe rufen, die Oka, Kama, Unscha, Wjetluga
Und ihre Enkelinnen, die Tschussowaja, die Wjatka.
Alle ihre Kräfte wird sie sammeln, mit den Wassern aus
    siebentausend Nebenflüssen
Wird sie sich zornerfüllt auf den Stalingrader Staudamm stürzen.
Dieses erfinderische Genie, mit dem teuflischen Spürsinn
Des Griechen Odysseus, wird alle Erdspalten ausnützen
Rechts ausbiegen, links vorbeigehn, unterm Boden
Sich verkriechen—aber, lese ich, die Sowjetmenschen
Die sie lieben, die sie besingen, haben sie
Neuerdings studiert und werden sie
Noch vor dem Jahre 1958
Bezwingen.

XV
READING HORACE

Even the Flood
Did not last for ever.
There came a time
When the black waters ebbed.
Yes, but how few
Have lasted longer!

XVI
SOUNDS

Later, in autumn
The white poplars harbor great swarms of rooks
But all summer long when
The region is birdless I hear
Only sounds of human provenance.
I have no objection.

XVII
READING A SOVIET BOOK

To tame the Volga, I read,
Will not be an easy task. She will call
On her daughters for help, on the Oka, Kama, Unsha, Vyetluga
And her granddaughters, the Tchussevaya, the Vyatka.
She'll summon all her forces, with waters from seven thousand
    tributaries
Full of rage she'll crash down on the Stalingrad dam.
That genius of invention, with the devilish cunning
Of the Greek Odysseus, will make use of every fissure
Deploy on the right flank, by-pass on the left, take cover
Underground—but, I read, the Soviet people
Who love her, sing songs about her, have lately
Studied her and no later
Than 1958
Will tame her.

Und die schwarzen Gefilde der Kaspischen Niederung
Die dürren, die Stiefkinder
Werden es ihnen mit Brot vergüten.

XVIII
DER HIMMEL DIESES SOMMERS

Hoch über dem See fliegt ein Bomber.
Von den Ruderbooten auf
Schauen Kinder, Frauen, ein Greis. Von weitem
Gleichen sie jungen Staren, die Schnäbel aufreissend
Der Nahrung entgegen.

XIX
DIE KELLE

Im Traum stand ich auf einem Bau. Ich war
Ein Maurer. In der Hand
Hielt ich eine Kelle. Aber als ich mich bückte
Nach dem Mörtel, fiel ein Schuss
Der riss mir von meiner Kelle
Das halbe Eisen.

XX
DIE MUSEN

Wenn der Eiserne sie prügelt
Singen die Musen lauter.
Aus gebläuten Augen
Himmeln sie ihn hündisch an.
Der Hintern zuckt vor Schmerz
Die Scham vor Begierde.

XXI
BEI DER LEKTÜRE EINES SPÄTGRIECHISCHEN DICHTERS

In den Tagen als ihr Fall gewiss war—
Auf den Mauern begann schon die Totenklage

And the black fields of the Caspian plains,
The arid, the stepchildren,
Will reward them with bread.

XVIII
THIS SUMMER'S SKY

High up above the lake a bomber flies.
From the rowing boats
Children look up, women, an old man. From a distance
They appear like young starlings, their beaks
Wide open for food.

XIX
THE TROWEL

In a dream I stood on a building site. I was
A bricklayer. In my hand
I held a trowel. But when I bent down
For cement, a shot rang out
That tore half the iron
Off my trowel.

XX
THE MUSES

When the brazen one beats them
The Muses sing louder.
With blackened eyes
They adore him like bitches.
Their buttocks twitch with pain
Their thighs with lust.

XXI
READING A LATE GREEK POET

At the time when their fall was certain—
On the ramparts the lament for the dead had begun—

Richteten die Troer Stückchen grade, Stückchen
In den dreifachen Holztoren, Stückchen.
Und begannen Mut zu haben und gute Hoffnung.

Auch die Troer also.

Ich benötige keinen Grabstein

Ich benötige keinen Grabstein, aber
Wenn ihr einen für mich benötigt
Wünschte ich, es stünde darauf:
Er hat Vorschläge gemacht. Wir
Haben sie angenommen.
Durch eine solche Inschrift wären
Wir alle geehrt.

Vergnügungen

Der erste Blick aus dem Fenster am Morgen
Das wiedergefundene alte Buch
Begeisterte Gesichter
Schnee, der Wechsel der Jahreszeiten
Die Zeitung
Der Hund
Die Dialektik
Duschen, Schwimmen
Alte Musik
Bequeme Schuhe
Begreifen
Neue Musik
Schreiben, Pflanzen
Reisen
Singen
Freundlich sein.

The Trojans adjusted small pieces, small pieces
In the triple wooden gate, small pieces
And began to take courage, to hope.

The Trojans too, then.

I Need No Gravestone

I need no gravestone, but
If you need one for me
I wish the inscription would read:
He made suggestions. We
Have acted on them.
Such an epitaph would
Honor us all.

Pleasures

Looking out of the window first thing in the morning
The old book found again
Enthusiastic faces
Snow, the alternation of seasons
The newspaper
The dog
Dialectics
Taking showers, swimming
Old music
Shoes that fit
Learning to understand
New music
Writing, planting
Travelling
Singing
Feeling kindly disposed.

Das Gewächshaus

Erschöpft vom Wässern der Obstbäume
Betrat ich neulich das kleine aufgelassene Gewächshaus
Wo im Schatten der brüchigen Leinwand
Die Überreste der seltenen Blumen liegen.

Noch steht aus Holz, Tuch und Blechgitter
Die Apparatur, noch hält der Bindfaden
Die bleichen verdursteten Stengel hoch
Vergangener Tage Sorgfalt
Ist noch sichtbar, mancher Handgriff. Am Zeltdach
Schwankt der Schatten der billigen Immergrüne
Die vom Regen lebend nicht der Kunst bedürfen.
Wie immer die schönen Empfindlichen
Sind nicht mehr.

Schwierige Zeiten

Stehend an meinem Schreibpult
Sehe ich durchs Fenster im Garten den Holderstrauch
Und erkenne darin etwas Rotes und etwas Schwarzes
Und erinnere mich plötzlich des Holders
Meiner Kindheit in Augsburg.
Mehrere Minuten erwäge ich
Ganz ernsthaft, ob ich zum Tisch gehn soll
Meine Brille holen, um wieder
Die schwarzen Beeren an den roten Zweiglein zu sehen.

Wechsel der Dinge

I
Und ich war alt, und ich war jung zu Zeiten
War alt am Morgen und am Abend jung
Und war ein Kind, erinnernd Traurigkeiten
Und war ein Greis ohne Erinnerung.

The Greenhouse

Exhausted with watering the fruit trees
The other day I entered the little greenhouse, left open,
Where in the shade of brittle canvas
Lie the remains of the rarer flowers.

Still the framework of wood, cloth and tin fencing
Holds, and string keeps upright
The pale dry stalks
The care of earlier times
Is visible still, many a trace of tending. On the canvas roof
Play the shadows of the cheap evergreens
Which, living on rain, need no human art.
As always the beautiful sensitive plants
Are no more.

Difficult Times

As I stand at my writing desk
Through the window I see the elder tree in the garden
And recognize something red in it, something black
And all at once recall the elder
Of my childhood in Augsburg.
For several minutes I debate
Quite seriously whether to go to the table
And pick up my spectacles, in order to see
Those black berries again on their tiny red stalks.

How Things Change

I
And I was old and I was young at times
Was old in the mornings, young at night
And was a child reliving childish griefs
And was an old man with no memory.

II
War traurig, wann ich jung war
Bin traurig, nun ich alt
So, wann kann ich mal lustig sein?
Es wäre besser bald.

Und ich dachte immer

Und ich dachte immer: die allereinfachsten Worte
Müssen genügen. Wenn ich sage, was ist
Muss jedem das Herz zerfleischt sein.
Dass du untergehst, wenn du dich nicht wehrst
Das wirst du doch einsehn.

Als ich in weissem Krankenzimmer der Charité

Als ich in weissem Krankenzimmer der Charité
Aufwachte gegen Morgen zu
Und die Amsel hörte, wusste ich
Es besser. Schon seit geraumer Zeit
Hatte ich keine Todesfurcht mehr. Da ja nichts
Mir je fehlen kann, vorausgesetzt
Ich selber fehle. Jetzt
Gelang es mir, mich zu freuen
Alles Amselgesanges nach mir auch.

II
Felt sad when I was young
Feel sad now that I'm old
Like that, when may I be merry for once?
It had better be soon.

And I Always Thought

And I always thought: the very simplest words
Must be enough. When I say what things are like
Everyone's heart must be torn to shreds.
That you'll go down if you don't stand up for yourself—
Surely you see that.

When in a White Ward of the Charité

When in a white ward of the Charité
I awoke around dawn
And heard the blackbird I knew
Better. For quite some time
I had not feared death. Since there is nothing
I can lack or miss, provided
I myself am missing. Now
What made me glad was different, including
The song of every blackbird after I am gone.

Peter Huchel
(b. 1903)

Das Zeichen

Baumkahler Hügel,
Noch einmal flog
Am Abend die Wildentenkette
Durch wässrige Herbstluft.

War es das Zeichen?
Mit falben Lanzen
Durchbohrte der See
Den ruhlosen Nebel.

Ich ging durchs Dorf
Und sah das Gewohnte.
Der Schäfer hielt den Widder
Gefesselt zwischen den Knien.
Er schnitt die Klaue,
Er teerte die Stoppelhinke.
Und Frauen zählten die Kannen,
Das Tagesgemelk.
Nichts war zu deuten.
Es stand im Herdbuch.

Nur die Toten,
Entrückt dem stündlichen Hall
Der Glocke, dem Wachsen des Epheus,
Sie sehen
Den eisigen Schatten der Erde
Gleiten über den Mond.
Sie wissen, dieses wird bleiben.
Nach allem, was atmet
In Luft und Wasser.

Wer schrieb
Die warnende Schrift,
Kaum zu entziffern?
Ich fand sie am Pfahl,
Dicht hinter dem See.
War es das Zeichen?

The Sign

Hill bare of trees,
Once again at evening
The flight of wild ducks passed
Through watery autumn air.

Was it the sign?
With pale yellow lances
The lake pierced
Unquiet mist.

I walked through the village
And saw what I expected.
The shepherd held a ram
Wedged between his knees.
He pared the hoof,
He tarred the stubble lameness.
And women counted the pails,
The day's milking.
There was nothing to interpret.
The accounts had been kept.

Only the dead,
Removed from the hourly stroke
Of the bell, the ivy's growth,
They see
The icy shadow of Earth
Slide over the moon.
They know that this will remain.
After all that breathes
In air and water.

Who wrote
The warning words,
Hardly to be deciphered?
I found them on the post,
Near the lake's far shore.
Was it the sign?

Erstarrt
Im Schweigen des Schnees,
Schlief blind
Das Kreuzotterndickicht.

Landschaft hinter Warschau

Spitzhackig schlägt der März
Das Eis des Himmels auf.
Es stürzt das Licht aus rissigem Spalt,
Niederbrandend
Auf Telegrafendrähte und kahle Chausseen.
Am Mittag nistet es weiss im Röhricht,
Ein grosser Vogel.
Spreizt er die Zehen, glänzt hell
Die Schwimmhaut aus dünnem Nebel.

Schnell wird es dunkel.
Flacher als ein Hundegaumen
Ist dann der Himmel gewölbt.
Ein Hügel raucht,
Als sässen dort noch immer
Die Jäger am nassen Winterfeuer.
Wohin sie gingen?
Die Spur des Hasen im Schnee
Erzählte es einst.

Momtschil

Mond kam über die Kimme der Berge.
Im Felsen ging das Silber auf,
Das Auge der Nacht.
Gedröhn von Hufen,
Langtönend im Stein,
Erstickte der Staub.
Schneller trieb die Herde der Hirt,
Sein Schatten erklomm
Das Schweigen der Schlucht.

Frozen in the silence of snow
The viper thicket
Blindly slept.

Landscape Beyond Warsaw

March with its sharp pick
Splits the ice of the sky.
From the cracks light pours
Billowing down
On to telegraph wires and bare main roads.
At noon white it roosts in the reeds,
A great bird.
When it spreads its claws, brightly
The webs gleam out of thin mist.

Nightfall is brief.
Then more shallow than a dog's palate
The sky arches.
A hill smokes
As though still the huntsmen
Were sitting there by the damp winter fire.
Where have they gone?
The hare's tracks in the snow
Once told us where.

Momtschil

Moon came over the ridges of the hills,
In the rocks the silver opened up,
The eye of night.
Thunder of hooves,
Long reverberation in the stones,
The dust was stifling.
The shepherd goaded his herd on,
His shadow climbed
The gully's silence.

Bergoben,
Umgürtet von felsiger Mauer,
Doch ausgesetzt
Dem Anhauch grosser Himmel,
Das Dorf der Tataren;
Die graue Moschee
Nicht höher als der Schober aus Stroh.
Neben dem Wasserrad die Hütte,
Der kühle, weiche Geruch von Mehl
Lag auf der Schwelle.
Und Nebel floss,
Weisse Schafsmilch,
Über den Rand des Dachs.

Der Spiegel

Am Abend versinken im Spiegel
Flut und Ebbe zuckender Lichter.
Schräg in die Erde
Geht der Mönch
Und deutet die Zeichen,
Geritzt in die Wand.
Es schwimmt der Fisch
Am Schleusentor des Himmels.

Auch brennt ein Feuer im Spiegel,
Das meine Hände einst wärmte.
Über den Sattelbogen des Passes
Der weiche gleitende Gang
Der Kamele. Und vor der Höhle,
Umweht vom Schatten
Treibenden Schnees,
Die Einsamkeit der Eule.

On the mountain,
Enclosed by a wall of rock
But exposed
To the breath of vast heavens,
The village of the Tartars;
The gray mosque
No higher than a haystack.
Next to the waterwheel the cottage,
The cool white smell of meal
Lay on the threshold.
And mist was flowing,
White sheep's milk,
Over the edge of the roof.

The Mirror

At evening ebb and flood
Of twitching lights sink in the mirror.
The monk walks
Obliquely into the earth
And interprets the signs
Scratched on the wall.
The fish swims
At the lock gate of the sky.

In the mirror there is also a fire burning
That once warmed my hands.
Across the saddlebow of the pass
The soft, gliding gait of camels.
And in front of the cave,
Blown round by the shadow
Of drifting snow,
The owl's loneliness.

Wei Dun und die alten Meister

Bewundernd die alten Meister,
Die Steine malten als Knochen der Erde
Und dünnen Nebel als Haut der Berge,
War ich bemüht, mit steilem Pinsel,
Mit schnellem und verweilendem Strich
Den feuchten Glanz des Regens zu tuschen.

Da aber Mond und Sonne beschienen
Mehr und mehr verwüstetes Land,
Lagen nicht Steine als Knochen der Erde—
Gebein von Menschen knirschte im Sand,
Wo Panzer rissen mit fressender Kette
Das graue Mark der Strassen bloss.

O alte Meister, ich schabte den Tuschstein.
Ich wusch die Pinsel aus Ziegenhaar.
Doch als ich streifte im Rücken des Feindes,
Sah ich die unbewässerten Felder,
Das Schöpfrad zerschossen, im harten Geschirr
Starr hängen den Ochsen am Göpel,
Die Tempelhalle, ausgeplündert,
Wo auf dem Schutt lasierter Kacheln
Im weissen Mittag die Schlange schlief.

O alte Meister, wie sollte ich tuschen
Die felsige Rückenflosse der Flüsse,
Als stünde lauernd im flachen Wasser
Ein riesiger Fisch mit Kiemen aus Sonne.
Und tuschen den kühlen Duft des Nebels,
Das graue Weiss der schwebenden Schneeluft,
Als flöge Flaum aus windigem Nest.

Wohin, wohin zog euer Himmel,
In welche Fernen, erlauchte Meister,
Der Hauch der Welt, so leicht verwundbar?
Bilder des Schreckens suchten mich heim
Und beizten das Auge mit Rauch und Trauer.

Wei Dun and the Old Masters

Marvelling at the old masters,
Who painted boulders as bones of the earth
And thin mists as the skin of hills,
I had tried, with vertical brush,
With quick strokes and slow ones,
To color the moist radiance of rain.

But as moon and sun shone
On land going more and more to ruin
It was not boulders that were the earth's bones—
Human bones were grinding in the sand
Where tanks ripped with guzzling tracks
Roads open to their gray marrow.

Old masters, I scraped the paint block,
I cleaned the brush of goat hair.
Yet as I rambled behind the foe
I saw the meadows waterless,
The mill wheel shattered, in hardened gear
The oxen hang rigid in the whim-shaft,
The temple porch plundered
Where on glazed tiles in a heap
The snake dozed all the white noon.

Old masters, how can I paint
The river's rocky dorsal fins
As if, in the shallows, there was lurking
Some giant fish with gills of sun.
And paint the cool bloom of the mist,
The gray whiteness of buoyant snowy air,
As if soft feathers floated from a windy nest.

Where, where have they gone, your heavens,
Into what distances, exalted masters,
The breath of the world, so vulnerable?
Images of terror visited me
And etched my eye with smoke and sorrow.

Wo bist du, „Flötespielender Schiffer"?
Blickst du im Regen den Wildgänsen nach?
Nachts ging ein Klagen über den Fluss.
Es harkte mit qualmendem Ast Dein Weib
In Glut und Asche der Bambushütte,
Um deinen schwarzen Schädel zu finden.

Und „Alter Mann, heimkehrend vom Dorffest",
Still durch die Kühle fallenden Taus
Auf deinem Wasserbüffel reitend,
Blieb nicht dein Diener erschrocken stehn
Und liess das Leitseil locker schleifen?
Du lenktest den Büffel hinter den Felsen.
Der Feind war schon vor deinem Tor.

Wo ist das „Gehöft am See", umweht
Vom Haar der Gräser und Bäume?
Und wo im Schnee, gefiltert durch Nebel,
Das einsame „Dorf im Hochgebirge"?
Suche hinter den Zäunen aus Feuer!
Ausgedörrt hat alles der Krieg
Auf dieser Darre des Todes.

Wo sind die Stimmen, das Gonggetöse,
Der Duft von Tusche, ihr Dichter und Maler
Der „Landschaft mit Gelehrten bevölkert"?
Wie liegt ihr stumm auf blachem Feld,
Beraubt der Schuhe, der Amulette
Und preisgegeben den Vögeln und Winden.

Himmel und Erde nähren
Noch immer die zehntausend Wesen.
Die Knochen modern in der Tiefe.
Der Atem aber steigt in die Höhe
Und fliesst als Licht, durch das ihr einst,
O alte Meister, in grosser Ruhe geschritten.

Where have you gone, Boatman Playing the Flute?
Do you watch in the rain the wild geese flying?
Over the river at night a moaning went.
Your wife with a smoking branch raked
Ashes and embers of your bamboo hut,
To discover there your blackened skull.

And Old Man Going Home from a Village Feast,
Quietly riding your water buffalo,
Through the coolness of falling dew,
Didn't your servant stop in horror
And let the rope loosely hang down?
You rode the buffalo behind the cliff.
By then the foe was at your door.

Where is the Farm by the Lake, fanned
By a chevelure of trees and grasses?
And where in the snow, filtered through mist,
The lonely Village in the High Mountains?
Search behind the penfold of the fire.
War has baked all things dry
In this kiln of death.

Where are the voices, noise of gongs,
The odor of pigment, you poets and painters
Of the Landscape Populated by Scholars?
Dumb, on the level field, how you lie,
Robbed of your shoes, your amulets,
Abandoned to the birds and winds.

Heaven and Earth sustain
Still the ten thousand things.
Deep down, the bones rot.
But the breath flies upward,
Flowing as light you walked through once,
Old masters, with great composure.

Unter der Kiefer

Nadeln ohne Öhr,
Der Nebel zieht
Die weissen Fäden ein.
Fischgräten,
In den Sand gescharrt.
Mit Katzenpfoten
Klettert der Epheu
Den Stamm hinauf.

Auffliegende Schwäne

Noch ist es dunkel, im Erlenkreis,
Die Flughaut nasser Nebel
Streift dein Kinn. Und in den See hinab,
Klaftertief,
Hängt schwer der Schatten.

Ein jähes Weiss,
Mit Füssen und Flügeln das Wasser peitschend,
Facht an den Wind. Sie fliegen auf,
Die winterbösen Majestäten.
Es pfeift metallen.
Duck dich ins Röhricht.
Schneidende Degen
Sind ihre Federn.

Hinter den Ziegelöfen

Erhabene Helle,
Noch zu finden im fauligen Licht
Gestauter Wasser. Hinter den Ziegelöfen,
Gleisentlang,
Die leichte Dünung der Gräser.
Biege das weisse Schilf zurück,

Under the Pine Tree

Needles without eyes.
The mist
Threads them with white cotton.
Fish bones
Lightly scratched into sand.
With cats' paws
Ivy
Climbs the trunk.

Swans Rising

It is still dark, in the circle of the alders
Membranes of wet mist
Streak past your chin. Shadows hang heavily,
Fathoms deep,
Down into the lake.

An abrupt whiteness
With feet and wings lashing the water
Beats at the air. They fly up,
Their winter-evil Majesties.
A metallic whistling.
Squat down in the reeds:
Their feathers cut like daggers.

Behind the Brick Kilns

Noble brightness
To be found in the putrid light
Of stagnant water even. Behind the brick kilns,
On either side of the rails,
A dunescape of rippled grasses.
Bend back the white reeds

Du stehst vor der Furt des Mittags.
Hier wird Gold gewaschen
Und auf zerbrochene Ziegel geschüttet.

Chausseen

Erwürgte Abendröte
Stürzender Zeit!
Chausseen. Chausseen.
Kreuzwege der Flucht.
Wagenspuren über den Acker,
Der mit den Augen
Erschlagener Pferde
Den brennenden Himmel sah.

Nächte mit Lungen voll Rauch,
Mit hartem Atem der Fliehenden,
Wenn Schüsse
Auf die Dämmerung schlugen.
Aus zerbrochenem Tor
Trat lautlos Asche und Wind,
Ein Feuer,
Das mürrisch das Dunkel kaute.

Tote,
Über die Gleise geschleudert,
Den erstickten Schrei
Wie einen Stein am Gaumen.
Ein schwarzes
Summendes Tuch aus Fliegen
Schloss ihre Wunden.

Bericht des Pfarrers vom Untergang seiner Gemeinde

Da Christus brennend sank vom Kreuz—o Todesgrauen!
Es schrien die erzenen Trompeten
Der Engel, fliegend im Feuersturm.
Ziegel wie rote Blätter wehten.

And you face the ford of noon.
Here gold is washed
And poured over broken bricks.

Roads

Choked sunset glow
Of crashing time.
Roads. Roads.
Intersections of flight.
Cart tracks across the ploughed field
That with the eyes
Of killed horses
Saw the sky in flames.

Nights with lungs full of smoke,
With the hard breath of the fleeing
When shots
Struck the dusk.
Out of a broken gate
Ash and wind came without a sound,
A fire
That sullenly chewed the darkness.

Corpses,
Flung over the rail tracks,
Their stifled cry
Like a stone on the palate.
A black
Humming cloth of flies
Closed their wounds.

The Pastor Reports on the Downfall of His Parish

When Christ sank burning from the cross—O terror of death!
The angels' brass trumpets shrilled
As they flew through the firestorm.
Tiles fluttered down like dead leaves.

Und heulend riss im wankenden Turm
Und Quadern schleudernd das Gemäuer,
Als berste des Erdballs Eisenkern.
O Stadt in Feuer!
O heller Mittag, in Schreie eingeschlossen—
Wie glimmendes Heu stob Haar der Frauen.
Und wo sie im Tiefflug auf Fliehende schossen,
Nackt und blutig lag die Erde, der Leib des Herrn.

Nicht war es der Hölle Sturz:
Knochen und Schädel wie gesteinigt
In grosser Wut, die Staub noch schmolz
Und mit dem erschrockenen Licht vereinigt
Brach Christi Haupt vom Holz.
Es schwenkten dröhnend die Geschwader.
Durch roten Himmel flogen sie ab,
Als schnitten sie des Mittags Ader.
Ich sah es schwelen, fressen, brennen—
Und aufgewühlt war noch das Grab.
Hier war kein Gesetz! Mein Tag war zu kurz,
Um Gott zu erkennen.

Hier war kein Gesetz. Denn wieder warf die Nacht
Aus kalten Himmeln feurige Schlacke.
Und Wind und Qualm. Und Dörfer wie Meiler angefacht.
Und Volk und Vieh auf enger Schneise.
Und morgens die Toten der Typhusbaracke,
Die ich begrub, von Grauen erfasst—
Hier war kein Gesetz. Es schrieb das Leid
Mit aschiger Schrift: Wer kann bestehn?
Denn nahe war die Zeit.

O öde Stadt, wie war es spät,
Es gingen die Kinder, die Greise
Auf staubigen Füssen durch mein Gebet.
Die löchrigen Strassen sah ich sie gehn.
Und wenn sie schwankten unter der Last
Und stürzten mit gefrorener Träne,
Nie kam im Nebel der langen Winterchausseen
Ein Simon von Kyrene.

And wailing in the shuddering tower, the walls,
Hurtling slabs of masonry, tore loose
As if earth's iron center had burst.
O city on fire!
O bright midday, besieged by screams—
Women's hair swirled round like gleaming hay
And where, diving low, they strafed the refugees,
Earth, the body of our Lord, lay naked and bloody.

It was not the fall of hell:
As if pelted by stones in a vast fury
That melted even dust, bones and skulls
And, at one with the startled light, Christ's head,
Broke from the wood.
The squadrons wheeled threateningly.
Through the red sky they flew off
As if they were slashing the arteries of noon.
I saw it smoldering, devouring, burning—
And graves, even graves, were churned up.
Here was no Law. My day had been too brief
To recognize God.

Here was no Law. For again night had cast
Fiery slag from the chill skies
And wind, and smoke. Villages were fanned like kilns,
People and cattle confined to a narrow fire-lane.
And in the mornings the dead of the typhus wards
Whom, clenched with horror, I buried.
Here was no Law. It was pain that wrote
With an ashen hand: Who can survive?
For the time was near.

O desolated city, how late it was,
The children were trudging and the old men
On dusty feet through my prayers.
Along the cratered streets I saw them go.
And whenever they swayed under the burden
And fell with a frozen tear
In the mist of the long winter highways
No Simon of Cyrene ever came.

Der Treck

Herbstprunk der Pappeln.
Und Dörfer
Hinter der Mauer
Aus Hundegeheul,
Am Torweg
Eingekeilt der Riegel,
Das Gold verborgen
Im rostigen Eisentopf.

Spät das letzte Gehöft.
Zerschossen trieb die Kettenfähre
Den Fluss hinab.

Hier sah ich das Kind,
Gebettet
In den kältesten Winkel der Stunde,
Aus der Höhle des Bluts
Ans Licht zersplitterter Fenster
Gestossen.
Das Kind war nahe dem Tag.

Draussen das Wasserloch
Ein Klumpen Eis.
Und Männer rissen mit Bajonetten
Fetzen Fleischs
Aus schneeverkrustetem Vieh,
Schleudernd den Abfall
Gegen die graubemörtelte
Mauer des Friedhofs.

Es kam die Nacht
Im krähentreibenden Nebel.
Hart ans Gehöft
Auf Krücken kahler Pappeln
Kam die Nacht.

Das Kind sah nicht
Die gräberhohle Erde.

The Trek

The autumnal flourish of poplars.
And villages walled in
By howling dogs,
At the gate
The bolt wedged fast,
The gold hidden
In the rusty iron pot.

Late the last farmstead.
Shot to bits, the chain ferry
Drifted downstream.

Here I saw the child
Embedded in the hour's coldest corner,
Thrust out from the caves of the blood
Into the light
Of shattered windows.
The child was near to day.

Outside the waterhole
A lump of ice.
And men with bayonets ripped
Tatters of meat
From snow-encrusted cattle,
Slinging the offal
Against the gray cemented
Wall of the churchyard.

Night came
In the crow-driving mist.
Suddenly to the farmstead
On crutches of bare poplars
Came the night.

The child saw neither
The earth hollowed with graves

Und nicht den Mond,
Der eine Garbe weissen Strohs
Auf Eis und Steine warf.
Das Kind war nahe dem Tag.

Die Pappeln

Zeit mit rostiger Sense,
Spät erst zogest du fort,
Den Hohlweg hinauf
Und an den beiden Pappeln vorbei.
Sie schwammen
Im dünnen Wasser des Himmels.
Ein weisser Stein ertrank.
War es der Mond, das Auge der Ödnis?

Am Gräbergebüsch die Dämmerung.
Sie hüllte ihr Tuch,
Aus Gras und Nebel grob gewebt,
Um Helme und Knochen.
Die erste Frühe, umkrustet von Eis,
Warf blinkende Scherben ins Schilf.
Schweigend schob der Fischer
Den Kahn in den Fluss. Es klagte
Die frierende Stimme des Wassers,
Das Tote um Tote flösste hinunter.

Wer aber begrub sie, im frostigen Lehm,
In Asche und Schlamm,
Die alte Fussspur der Not?
Im Kahlschlag des Kriegs glänzt Ackererde,
Es drängt die quellende Kraft des Halms.
Und wo der Schälpflug wendet,
Die Stoppel stürzt,
Stehn auf dem Hang die beiden Pappeln.
Sie ragen ins Licht
Als Fühler der Erde.

Nor the moon which threw
A sheaf of winter straw
On ice and stones.
The child was near to day.

The Poplars

Time with your rusty scythe,
Late you went on your way,
Up the narrow path
And past the two poplars.
They swam
In the sky's thin water.
A white stone drowned.
Was it the moon, desolation's eye?

Dusk on the graveside bushes.
It wound its cloth
Coarsely woven of grass and mist
Around helmets and bones.
The dawn light, encrusted with ice,
Threw glinting shards into rushes.
In silence the fisherman pushed
His boat into the river. The water's
Freezing voice complained,
Bearing corpse after corpse downstream.

But who buried them in the frosty clay,
In ashes and mud,
Disaster's old footprints?
Amid the razing impact of war
The ploughed field glistens, the corn blade's power wells up.
And where the paring plough turns,
Where stubble falls,
On the slope the two poplars remain.
They loom into light
As the antennae of Earth.

Schön ist die Heimat,
Wenn über der grünen Messingscheibe
Des Teichs der Kranich schreit
Und das Gold sich häuft
Im blauen Oktobergewölbe;
Wenn Korn und Milch in der Kammer schlafen,
Sprühen die Funken
Vom Amboss der Nacht.
Die russige Schmiede des Alls
Beginnt ihr Feuer zu schüren.
Sie schmiedet
Das glühende Eisen der Morgenröte.
Und Asche fällt
Auf den Schatten der Fledermäuse.

Winterquartier

Ich sitze am Schuppen
Und öle mein Gewehr.

Ein streunendes Huhn
Drückt mit dem Fuss
Zart in den Schnee
Weltalte Schrift,
Weltaltes Zeichen,
Zart in den Schnee
Den Lebensbaum.

Ich kenne den Schlächter
Und seine Art zu töten.
Ich kenne das Beil.
Ich kenne den Hauklotz.

Schräg durch den Schuppen
Wirst du flattern,
Kopfloser Rumpf,
Doch Vogel noch,
Der seinen zuckenden Flügel presst
Jäh ans gespaltene Holz.

Lovely our homeland is
When over the green brass disc
Of the pond a crane cries
And gold gathers
In October's blue vault;
When corn and milk sleep in the store-room
The sparks fly up
From night's anvil.
The world's sooty forge
Begins to fan its fire.
It beats out
The glowing iron of dawn.
And ash falls
On the shadows of bats.

Winter Billet

I sit by the shed,
Oiling my rifle.

A foraging hen
With her foot imprints
Lightly on snow
A script as old as the world,
A sign as old as the world,
Lightly on snow
The tree of life.

I know the butcher
And his way of killing.
I know the axe.
I know the chopping-block.

Across the shed
You will flutter,
Stump with no head,
Yet still a bird
That presses a twitching wing
Down on the split wood.

Ich kenne den Schlächter.
Ich sitze am Schuppen
Und öle mein Gewehr.

An taube Ohren der Geschlechter

Es war ein Land mit hundert Brunnen.
Nehmt für zwei Wochen Wasser mit.
Der Weg ist leer, der Baum verbrannt.
Die Öde saugt den Atem aus.
Die Stimme wird zu Sand
Und wirbelt hoch und stützt den Himmel
Mit einer Säule, die zerstäubt.

Nach Meilen noch ein toter Fluss.
Die Tage schweifen durch das Röhricht
Und reissen Wolle aus den schwarzen Kerzen.
Und eine Haut aus Grünspan schliesst
Das Wasserloch,
Als faule Kupfer dort im Schlamm.

Denk an die Lampe
Im golddurchwirkten Zelt des jungen Afrikanus:
Er liess ihr Öl nicht länger brennen,
Denn Feuer wütete genug,
Die siebzehn Nächte zu erhellen.

*

Polybios berichtet von den Tränen,
Die Scipio verbarg im Rauch der Stadt.
Dann schnitt der Pflug
Durch Asche, Bein und Schutt.
Und der es aufschrieb, gab die Klage
An taube Ohren der Geschlechter.

I know the butcher.
I sit by the shed,
Oiling my rifle.

To the Deaf Ears of Generations

It was a land of a hundred springs.
Take two weeks' supply of water with you,
The road is empty, the trees are burnt down.
The solitude sucks your breath away.
Your voice becomes sand,
Swirls up and supports the heavens
With a column that turns to dust.

Miles later another dead river.
The days range through the reeds
And snatch wool from the black candles.
A skin of verdigris seals off
The water hole,
As though copper were rotting down there in the mud.

Think of the lamp
In the gold-embroidered tent of Africanus:
He did not let its oil burn any longer,
With fire enough raging
To illumine the seventeen nights.

                              *

Polybios tells of the tears
That Scipio could conceal through the city's smoke.
Then the plough sheared
Through ashes, rubble, bone.
And he who wrote it down bequeathed his lament
To the deaf ears of generations.

Der Garten des Theophrast

Meinem Sohn

Wenn mittags das weisse Feuer
Der Verse über den Urnen tanzt,
Gedenke, mein Sohn. Gedenke derer,
Die einst Gespräche wie Bäume gepflanzt.
Tot ist der Garten, mein Atem wird schwerer,
Bewahre die Stunde, hier ging Theophrast,
Mit Eichenlohe zu düngen den Boden,
Die wunde Rinde zu binden mit Bast.
Ein Ölbaum spaltet das mürbe Gemäuer
Und ist noch Stimme im heissen Staub.
Sie gaben Befehl, die Wurzel zu roden.
Es sinkt dein Licht, schutzloses Laub.

Psalm

Dass aus dem Samen des Menschen
Kein Mensch
Und aus dem Samen des Ölbaums
Kein Ölbaum
Werde,
Es ist zu messen
Mit der Elle des Todes.

Die da wohnen
Unter der Erde
In einer Kugel aus Zement,
Ihre Stärke gleicht
Dem Halm
Im peitschenden Schnee.

Die Öde wird Geschichte.
Termiten schreiben sie
Mit ihren Zangen
In den Sand.

The Garden of Theophrastus

To my son

When at noon the white fire of verses
Flickering dances above the urns,
Remember, my son. Remember the vanished
Who planted their conversations like trees.
The garden is dead, more heavy my breathing,
Preserve the hour, here Theophrastus walked,
With oak bark to feed the soil and enrich it,
To bandage with fiber the wounded bole.
And olive tree splits the brickwork grown brittle
And still is a voice in the mote-laden heat.
Their order was to fell and uproot it,
Your light is fading, defenceless leaves.

Psalm

That from the seed of men
No man
And from the seed of the olive tree
No olive tree
Shall grow,
This you must measure
With the yardstick of death.

Those who live
Under the earth
In a capsule of cement,
Their strength is like
A blade of grass
Lashed by snow in a blizzard.

The desert now will be history.
Termites with their pincers
Write it
On sand.

Und nicht erforscht wird werden
Ein Geschlecht,
Eifrig bemüht,
Sich zu vernichten.

And no one will enquire
Into a species
Eagerly bent
On self-extinction.

Johannes Bobrowski
(1917–1965)

Im Strom

Mit den Flössen hinab
im helleren Grau des fremden
Ufers, einem
Glanz, der zurücktritt, dem Grau
schräger Flächen, aus Spiegeln
beschoss uns das Licht.

Es lag des Täufers Haupt
auf der zerrissenen Schläfe,
in das verschnittene Haar
eine Hand mit bläulichen, losen
Nägeln gekrallt.

Als ich dich liebte, unruhig
dein Herz, die Speise auf schlagendem
Feuer, der Mund, der sich öffnete,
offen, der Strom
war ein Regen und flog
mit den Reihern, Blätter
fielen und füllten sein Bett.

Wir beugten uns über erstarrte
Fische, mit Schuppen bekleidet
trat der Grille Gesang
über den Sand, aus den Lauben
des Ufers, wir waren gekommen
einzuschlafen, Niemand
umschritt das Lager, Niemand
löschte die Spiegel, Niemand
wird uns wecken
zu unserer Zeit.

Mitternachtsdorf

Im verwinkelten Himmel
mit schwerem Fuss

Midstream

Drifting down with the rafts,
in the lighter gray of the strange
shore, in a
splendor, which withdraws, in the gray
of slanting surfaces, light
shot at us from mirrors.

The Baptist's head
lay on its torn brow,
a hand with loose bluish
nails clawing
the ragged hair.

When I loved you restless
your heart, the food on the beating
fire, your mouth, which opened,
open, the river
was a rain and flew
with the herons, leaves
fell and filled its bed.

We bent over numbed
fish, the cricket's song,
clad in scales, crossed
the sand from the foliage
of the bank, we had come
to sleep. Noman
circled the bed. Noman
extinguished the mirrors, Noman
will wake us
in our time.

Midnight Village

In the many-angled sky
Saturn plods with heavy feet

tappt durch den Schatten Saturn
und pfeift seinen Monden.

Aus dem zerbrochnen Dach
wär es zu sehen, aber
das Haus ganz voll von Schlaf
wie von Wäldern
rührt sich im Schlaf,
auf seinem Atem mit offenen
Flügeln schlafen die Vögel.

Lass uns schlafen einer
des andern Schlaf und hören
nicht die Sterne und alle
Stinmen im Finstren, das Blut
nur wie es fällt und zurücksinkt
mit rotgeränderten, schwärzlichen
Blättern unter das Herz.

Morgen magst du verstreun
Asche über den Himmel,
vor die näherkommenden
Schritte Saturns.

Der lettische Herbst

Das Tollkirschendickicht
ist geöffnet, er tritt
auf die Lichtung, vergessen wird
um die Birkenstümpfe der Hühnertanz, er geht
vorüber am Baum, den die Reiher umflogen, auf Wiesen,
er hat gesungen.

Ach dass der Schwaden Heu,
wo er lag in der hellen Nacht,
das Heu zerstreut mit den Winden
flög auf den Ufern—

through the shadows
and whistles his moons.

It could have been seen
through the broken roof, but
the house full of sleep
like the sleep of forests
stirs in sleep,
the birds sleep on its breath
with open wings.

Let us sleep each
other's sleep and not
hear the stars and all the
voices in the darkness, the blood
only as it falls and sinks back
with red-edged, blackish
leaves under the heart.

In the morning you may strew
ashes across the sky
before the approaching
footsteps of Saturn.

The Latvian Autumn

The thicket of deadly nightshade
is open, he steps
into the clearing, the dance
of the hens around the birch stumps is forgotten, he walks
past the tree round which the herons flew, he has sung
in the meadows.

Oh that the swath of hay,
where he lay in the bright night,
might fly scattered by winds
on the banks—

wenn nicht mehr wach ist der Strom,
die Wolke über ihm, Stimme
der Vögel, Rufe:
Wir kommen nicht mehr—

Dann entzünd ich dein Licht,
das ich nicht sehn kann, die Hände
legt' ich darüber, dicht
um die Flamme, sie blieb
stehen rötlich vor lauter Nacht
(wie die Burg, die herabkam
über den Hang zerfallen,
wie mit Flügeln das Schlänglein
Licht durch den Strom, wie das Haar
des Judenkindes)
und brannte mich nicht.

Schattenland

Die Raschelstimmen,
Blätter, Vögel, drei Wege
kamn ich
vor einem grossen Schnee.
Auf dem Ufer, Grannen und Kletten
im Ringelhaar, mit ihren Hunden
Ragana schrie nach dem Fährmann, im Wasser
stand er, mitten im Fluss.

Einmal,
folgend den Nebeln,
über die Senke mit goldenen Flügeln
zogen die Trappen, sie setzten
auf die Gräser den hornigen Fuss,
Licht flog, der Tag ihnen nach.

Kalt. Auf der Spitze des Grashalms
die Leere weiss
bis an den Himmel. Der Baum
aber alt, dort ist

when the river is no longer awake,
the clouds above it, voices
of birds, calls:
We shall come no more.

Then I light your light,
which I cannot see, I placed
my hands above it, close
round the flame, it stood still,
reddish in nothing but night
(like the castle which fell
in ruins over the slope,
like the little winged snake
of light through the river, like the hair
of the Jewish child)
and did not burn me.

Shadowland

The rustling voices,
leaves, birds, I came
three ways
before a great snow.
On the bank, burrs and awns
in her ringlets, Ragana with her hounds
shouted for the ferryman, he stood
in the water, midstream.

Once,
following the mists
across the dell with golden wings,
the bustard flew, they set
horny feet on the grass,
light, the day, flew after them.

Cold. On the tip of a grass-blade
the emptiness, white,
reaching to the sky. But the tree
old, there is

ein Ufer, Nebel mit dünnen
Gelenken gehn auf dem Fluss.

Finsternis, wer hier lebt,
spricht mit des Vogels Stimme.
Ausgefahren sind
Windlichter über den Wäldern.
Kein Atem hat sie bewegt.

An Klopstock

Wenn ich das Wirkliche nicht
wollte, dieses: ich sag
Strom und Wald,
ich hab in die Sinne aber
gebunden die Finsternis,
Stimme des eilenden Vogels, den Pfeilstoss
Licht um den Abhang

und die tönenden Wasser—
wie wollt ich
sagen deinen Namen,
wenn mich ein kleiner Ruhm
fände—ich hab
aufgehoben, dran ich vorüberging,
Schattenfabel von den Verschuldungen
und der Sühnung:
so als den Taten
trau ich—du führtest sie—trau ich
der Vergesslichen Sprache,
sag ich hinab in die Winter
ungeflügelt, aus Röhricht
ihr Wort.

a shore, mists with thin
bones move on the river.

Darkness, whoever lives here
speaks with the bird's voice.
Lanterns have glided
above the forests.
No breath has moved them.

To Klopstock

If I did not want
what is real, this: I say
river and forest,
but I have woven
into my senses the darkness,
voice of the hastening bird, the bowshot
of light round the slope

and the sounding waters—
how would I
speak your name
if a small fame
found me—I have
gathered what I passed,
the shadowed fable of guilt
and atonement:
just as the deeds
I trust—you guided it—I trust
the language of those who forget,
down into the winters, unwinged,
from the reeds, I speak
its word.

Erfahrung

Zeichen,
Kreuz und Fisch,
an die Steinwand geschrieben der Höhle.

Die Prozession der Männer
taucht hinab in die Erde.
Der Boden wölbt sich herauf,
Kraut, grünlich, gewachsen
durch ein Gesträuch.

Gegen die Brust
steht mir der Strom auf,
die Stimme aus Sand:

öffne dich
ich kann nicht hindurch
deine toten
treiben in mir

Herberge

Licht, herab
mit des Klettenblatts
Neigung, die Zeile Licht—
Wind, der gläserne Flügel
rührt auf dem Ufer.

Komm und geh und kehr wieder,
komm und bleib, ein Haus,
Nebelhaus, steht vor dem Wald,
Dächer aus Rauch,
Türme aus Vogelrufen,
Birkenzweige abends verschliessen die Tür.

Experience

Signs,
cross and fish,
drawn on the stone wall of a cave.

The procession of men
descends into the earth.
The ground vaults,
weed, greenish, grown
through the bushes.

The river rises
against my breast,
the voice of sand:

open
I can not get through
your dead
drift in me

Sanctuary

Light, falling
with a curve
of the burdock leaf, the line of light—
wind, the glassy wing
stirs on the bank.

Come and go and come again,
come and stay, a house,
a house of mist, stands before the forest,
roofs of smoke,
towers of birdcalls,
birch branches secure the door at evening.

Ruhlos liegen wir dort,
Schattentuch auf der Schulter,
um die Fischerfeuer
gehn mit den rötlichen Flossen
die Lüfte, du sprichst, fremde Stimme,
ich hör dich mit fremdem Ohr.

Die Wolgastädte

Der Mauerstrich.
Türme. Die Stufe des Ufers. Einst,
die hölzerne Brücke zerriss. Über die Weite fuhren
Tatarenfeuer. Mit strähnigem Bart
Nacht, ein Wandermönch, kam
redend. Die Morgen
schossen herauf, die Zisternen
standen im Blut.

Geh umher auf dem Stein.
Hier im gläsernen Mittag
über die Augen hob
Minin die Hand. Dann Geschrei
stob herauf, den Wassern entgegen, Stjenkas
Ankunft—Es gehn auf dem Ufer
bis an die Hüften im Unterholz
Sibiriaken, ihre
Wälder ziehn ihnen nach.

Dort
einen Menschenmund
hörte ich rufen:
Komm in dein Haus
durch die vermauerte Tür,
die Fenster schlag auf
gegen das Lichtmeer.

Restless we lie there,
a shawl of shadows on our shoulders,
the breezes move round
the fishermen's fires
with reddish fins,
you speak, alien voice,
I hear you with alien ear.

The Volga Towns

The stretch of wall.
Towers. The slope of the bank. Once
the wooden bridge broke. Tartar fires moved
through the plains. Night came talking,
a wandering friar with a straggly
beard. The mornings
leapt up, the cisterns
stood full of blood.

Walk about on the stone.
Here in the glassy noon
Minin raised his hand
to shade his eyes. Then shouts
flew up, toward the water, Stenka's
arrival—The Siberians walk
on the bank, up to their waists
in the undergrowth, their
forests follow them.

There
I heard
a human mouth calling:
Come into your house
through the bricked-up door,
fling open the windows
against the sea of light.

Mit deiner Stimme

Mit deiner Stimme
bis in die Nacht
redet der Weidenbusch, Lichter
fliegen um ihn.
Hoch, eine Wasserblume
fährt durch die Finsternis.
Mit seinen Tieren
atmet der Fluss.

In den Kalmus
trage ich mein geflochtenes Haus.
Die Schnecke
unhörbar
geht über mein Dach.
Eingezeichnet
in meine Handflächen
finde ich dein Gesicht.

Das Ende der Sommernacht

Der Distelkopf
schlägt nach den Lichtern
über dem Wasser. Ein Vogel
hat Zeichen geschrieben
ins Eschenlaub. Um die Wurzeln
von Schilf und Rohr
legt aus der Fisch sein Flossenrot.

Aufgestanden ist
gegen den Ruhm
der Staub.
Er, aus den Säulen der Nebel.
tritt in die Ebenen, über
die Flüsse, dunkel
rührt er die Feuer an.

With Your Voice

The willow bush speaks
with your voice
late into the night, lights
fly round it.
High, a water flower
moves through the darkness.
The river breathes
with its creatures.

Into the calamus
I carry my plaited house.
The snail,
inaudible,
moves across my roof.
Inscribed
upon my palms
I find your face.

The End of the Summer Night

The head of the thistle
strikes at the lights
above the water. A bird
has drawn signs
into the ash leaves. Around roots
of rush and reed
the fish spreads the red of its fins.

Dust
has risen
against fame.
Dust steps from the pillars
of mist into the plains, across
the rivers, dark
it touches the fires.

Kalmus

Mit Regensegeln umher
fliegt, ein Geheul,
der Wasserwind.
Eine blaue Taube
hat die Flügel gebreitet
über den Wald.
Schön im zerbrochenen Eisen
der Farne
geht das Licht
mit dem Kopf eines Fasans.

Atem,
ich sende dich aus,
find dir ein Dach,
geh ein durch ein Fenster, im weissen
Spiegel erblick dich,
dreh dich lautlos,
ein grünes Schwert.

Sprache

Der Baum
grösser als die Nacht
mit dem Atem der Talseen
mit dem Geflüster über
der Stille

Die Steine
unter dem Fuss
die leuchtenden Adern
lange im Staub
für ewig

Sprache
abgehetzt
mit dem müden Mund
auf dem endlosen Weg
zum Hause des Nachbarn

Calamus

The water-wind, a howl,
flies around
with sails of rain.
A blue dove
has spread its wings
across the wood.
Lovely in the broken iron
of the fern
the light moves
with the head of a pheasant.

Breath,
I send you out,
find a roof,
enter through a window, regard
yourself in the white mirror,
turn without sound,
a green sword.

Language

The tree
greater than the night
with the breath of the valley lakes
with the whisper above
the stillness

The stones
beneath the feet
the shining veins
long in the dust
for ever

Language
worn out
with the weary mouth
on the endless road
to the neighbor's house

Im leeren Spiegel

In den Gewässern des Lichts,
die Stirnen, gegeneinander,
Sommergehölz fliegt herauf
über die Hüfte dir, Blitze
schrei ich herab, ihr kommt
fernher, Blitze, Asche,
Flocken Asche
fallen von dir, dein Kleid.

An der Schulter war ich,
die Ader an deinem Hals
brach mir im Mund, du sinkst
nicht, ich halt dich
bei den Armen, ich heb
über die Tiefe dich, so
geh vor mir her.

Einmal: ich bring dir wieder
den Trunk, vor den Himmeln
flieg ich, einmal: ich komm
aber herab, du hörst mich
atmen, dich hören die Felder
über dem Wind, ein weisses
Licht spricht mit dir.

Wenn verlassen sind

Wenn verlassen sind
die Räume, in denen Antworten erfolgen, wenn
die Wände stürzen und Hohlwege, aus den Bäumen
fliegen die Schatten, wenn aufgegeben ist
unter den Füssen das Gras,
weiss Sohlen betreten den Wind—

der Dornbusch flammt,
ich hör seine Stimme,

In the Empty Mirror

In the waters of light,
the brows, against each other,
the summer undergrowth
springs up above your hips, I
call down lightnings, you come
from afar, lightnings, ashes,
flakes of ash
fall from you, your gown.

I was at your shoulder,
the vein on your neck
broke in my mouth, you
will not sink, I hold you
by the arms, I lift
you across the deep,
walk ahead of me.

One day: I shall bring you
the drink again, I shall fly
against the skies, one day: but I shall
descend, you will hear me
breathing, the fields will hear you
above the wind, a white light
will speak to you.

When the Rooms

When the rooms are deserted
in which answers are given, when
the walls and narrow passes fall, shadows
fly out of the trees, when the grass
beneath the feet is abandoned,
white soles tread the wind—

the bush of thorn flames,
I hear its voice,

wo keine Frage war, ein Gewässer
geht, doch mich dürstet nicht.

Feuerstelle

Wir sahn jenen Himmel. Schwärze
fuhr auf dem Strom, die Feuer
schlugen, mit zitternden Lichtern
vor den Uferwald trat
Finsternis, im Tierfell.
Wir hörten
die Münder im Laub.

Dieser Himmel stand
unbewegt. Und war
aus Stürmen und riss uns vornüber,
schreiend sahn wir die Erde
hinaufgehn mit Feldern und Strömen,
Wald, die fliegenden Feuer
erstarrt.

Tief blieb der Strom. Dei Schärfe
zog herauf der feuchten
Gräser. Die Grillenstimme
erhob sich im Rücken, es war
ein Baum uns im Rücken,
der Faulbaum.

Wir sahen den Himmel, der
verging in der Finsternis, Himmel
der Felder und fliegender alter
Gehölze. Es kamen Schritte
über das Moor, die Feuer
traten sie aus.

where no question was, the waters
move, but I do not thirst.

Place of Fire

We saw that sky. Blackness
moved on the water, the fires
beat, darkness with trembling
lights stepped forward in front
of the wood on the bank, in animal hide.
We heard
the mouths in the foliage.

That sky stood
unmoved. And was made
of storms and tore us forward,
screaming we saw the earth
ascending with fields and rivers,
forest, the flying fires
benumbed.

The river remained deep. The pungence
of damp grass
rose. The voice of the cricket
lifted behind us, there was
a tree behind us,
the black alder.

We saw the sky that
perished in the darkness, sky
of fields and flying ancient
groves. Steps came
across the marsh, they
stamped out the fires.

Vogelnest

Mein Himmel
wechselt mit deinem,
auch meine Taube
jetzt
überfliegt die deine,
ich seh zwei Schatten
fallen
im Haferfeld.

Wir vertauschen
unsere Augen,
wir finden
ein Lager:
Regen,
wir sagen
wie eine Geschichte
die halben Sätze
Grün,
ich hör:

Zu meiner Braue
hinauf
mit Vogelreden
dein Mund
trägt Federn und Zweige.

Jakub Bart in Ralbitz

Eulenschreie—
so in der Nacht
reden die Dörfer, wie sag ich,
dass ihr mich hört,

Bird's Nest

My sky
interchanges with yours,
so does my dove
now
it flies over yours,
I see two shadows
falling
in the oat field.

We look with
each other's eyes,
we find
a place:
rain
we say
like a story
the half-sentence
green,
I hear:

Your mouth
with the speech
of birds
carries twigs and feathers
up to my brow.

*Jakub Bart in Ralbitz

Owl cries—
thus the villages
talk in the night, how shall I speak
that you may hear me,

* Author's note: Jakub Bart-Cisinski (1856–1919), the Sorbian national
poet. He came as curate in Spring 1883 to Ralbitz, "the poorest parish in the
world". The quotation is a free translation of two lines of his poem "O tempora
o mores".

Sorben, es kommen die Fremden,
sie sagen:
ihr seid Tote, ihr seid
wenige, lernt zu schweigen,
streckt euch ins Grab.

Wacht doch,
dass ihr vernehmt
die Brüder hinter der Grenze,
über den Bergen wie Feuer,
über den Wäldern, es gehn
die Stürme
brüderlich, ihr hört:
sie reden mit eueren Mündern,
sie treten wie ihr die Erde,
sie gehn aus den Gruben
herauf wie ihr.

Aber wer,
dass ich rede,
bin ich geworden?
„Wehe, Stern, du bist
gefallen in Finsternis,
in das Getöse
aus blauer Höhe, der Höhe
ohne Laut"—
dorthinauf
erheb ich mich, es erhebt mich,
das seine Stimme gewann,
mein Volk.

Antwort

Über dem Zaun
deine Rede:
Von den Bäumen fällt die Last,
der Schnee.

Sorbs, the strangers are coming,
they say:
you are dead, you are
few, learn to be silent,
lie down in your graves.

But awake
that you may hear
your brothers beyond the border,
above the hills like fire,
above the forests, the storms
range
fraternally, you hear:
they talk with your mouths,
they walk the earth like you,
like you they come up
from the pits.

But who
have I become
that I speak?
"Woe, star, you have
fallen into darkness,
into the uproar
from the blue height, the height
without sound"—
I lift myself
to that height,
I am lifted by my people
that found its voice.

Answer

Above the fence
your talk:
From the trees the burden falls,
the snow.

Auch im gestürzten Holunder
das Schwirrlied der Amseln, der Grille
Gräserstimme
kerbt Risse ins Mauerwerk, Schwalbenflug
steil
gegen den Regen, Sternbilder
gehn auf dem Himmel,
im Reif.

Die mich einscharren
unter die Wurzeln,
hören:
er redet,
zum Sand,
der ihm den Mund füllt—so wird
reden der Sand, und wird
schreien der Stein, und wird
fliegen das Wasser.

Namen für den Verfolgten

Der hereinkommt,
im verhängten Fenster
spricht er die Namen nach,
die ich ihm gebe.
Vogelnamen und
den Namen des Raubaals.

gerwe sagt er
wie eine Kranichfeder die Luft streicht,
angurys wie unter der Wasserfläche
ein Schatten sich naht.

Zuletzt gebe ich ihm
den Namen Holunder, den
Namen des Unhörbaren, der
reif geworden ist
und steht voll Blut.

And in the fallen elder
the trilling of blackbirds, the crickets'
grassy voice
notches chinks into the wall. Swallow flight
steep against the rain, constellations
move into the sky,
in the hoarfrost.

They that bury me
beneath the roots
will hear:
he speaks
to the sand
that fills his mouth—so the sand
will speak, and
the stone will cry
and the water fly.

Names for the Persecuted

He who enters
repeats in the curtained window
the names that I give him,
names of birds and the name of the preying eel.

gerwe he says
like a crane's feather stroking the air,
angurys like a shadow approaching
under the water.

In the end I give him
the name "Eldertree", the name
of the inaudible, which
has ripened
and is full of blood.

Author's note: The two Old Prussian (Pruzzian) words mean: gerwe =
crane; angurys = eel, the so-called broadheaded eel.

Eszther

Das ist
mein Volk.
Das sich zerstreut
unter die Völker
und sitzt im Tor.

Auf den Steinen
der Wildgesichtige
richtet sich auf, die Länder
lässt er ruhen, das Gold
geht mit Flammen
über sein Haupt, er hört mich:

Komme ich um,
so komme ich um, ich erschrak,
deine Herrlichkeit mit
Blitzen jagt durch den Himmel,
das springende Blut
der Trompeten
baut mein Haus.

Das verlassene Haus

Die Allee
eingegrenzt
mit Schritten Verstorbener. Wie das Echo
über die Luftsee herab
kam, auf dem Waldgrund zieht
Efeu, die Wurzeln
treten hervor, die Stille
naht mit Vögeln, weissen Stimmen.
Im Haus
gingen Schatten, ein fremdes Gespräch
unter dem Fenster. Die Mäuse
huschen

Esther

This is
my people.
Which disperses
among the peoples
and sits at the gate.

The wild-faced one
stands erect
on the stones, he lets
the lands rest, the gold
moves with flames
above his head, he hears me:

If I perish
I perish, I was afraid,
your glory runs
with lightnings through the sky,
the leaping blood
of trumpets
builds my house.

The Deserted House

The avenue
defined
by the footsteps of the dead. How the echo
descended over the sea
of air, beneath the trees
ivy creeps, the roots
show, the silence
approaches with birds, white voices.
In the house
walked shadows, a strange conversation
beneath the window. The mice
scurry

durch das gesprungne Spinett.
Ich sah eine alte Frau
am Ende der Strasse
im schwarzen Tuch
auf dem Stein,
den Blick nach Süden gerichtet.
Über dem Sand
mit zerspaltenen harten Blättern
blühte die Distel.
Dort war der Himmel
aufgetan, in der Farbe des Kinderhaars.
Schöne Erde Vaterland.

through the broken spinet.
I saw an old woman
at the end of the road
in a black shawl
on the stone
she looked southward.
Above the sand
with hard split leaves
the thistle bloomed.
There the sky was
open, in the color of a child's hair.
Beautiful earth fatherland.

Günter Kunert
(b. 1929)

Unterschiede

Betrübt höre ich einen Namen aufrufen:
Nicht den meinigen.

Aufatmend
Höre ich einen Namen aufrufen:
Nicht den meinigen.

Über einige Davongekommene

Als der Mensch
Unter den Trümmern
Seines
Bombardierten Hauses
Hervorgezogen wurde,
Schüttelte er sich
Und sagte:
Nie wieder.

Jedenfalls nicht gleich.

Laika

In einer Kugel aus Metall,
Dem besten, das wir besitzen,
Fliegt Tag für Tag ein toter Hund
Um unsre Erde
Als Warnung,
Dass so einmal kreisen könnte
Jahr für Jahr um die Sonne,
Beladen mit einer toten Menschheit,
Der Planet Erde,
Der beste, den wir besitzen.

Differences

Distressed, I hear a name called out:
Not mine.

Relieved,
I hear a name called out:
Not mine.

On Certain Survivors

When the man
Was dragged out from under
The debris
Of his shelled house,
He shook himself
And said:
Never again.

At least, not right away.

Laika

In a capsule of metal,
The best that we have,
Day after day around our earth
A dead dog rotates
As a warning
That so in the end
With a cargo of human corpses
Year after year around the sun
This planet Earth could rotate,
The best that we have.

Durch Nichts sonst

Als nur durch
Eine einmalige allgewaltige Ätze
Die überall über alles sich ergiesst und auflöst
Alle Grösse
Und hierorts ZEIT heisst wird der Mensch
Zu Flecken auf seinen Möbeln die
Ihn besassen.

Langsam verdaut
Von den Eingeweiden seiner Wohnung
Zieht die geringe Wärme
Kurzen Daseins
In das Gestein hinter der Tapete bis
Er
Nicht mehr ist was er ist sondern
Ein undeutlicher Geruch seines Hauses
Und nicht mehr vorstellbar:
Jener besondre Jedermann.

Auf der Schwelle des Hauses

In den Dünen sitzen. Nichts sehen
Als Sonne. Nichts fühlen als
Wärme. Nichts hören
Als Brandung. Zwischen zwei
Herzschlägen glauben: Nun
Ist Frieden.

Film—verkehrt eingespannt

Als ich erwachte
Erwachte ich im atemlosen Schwarz
Der Kiste. Ich hörte: Die Erde tat sich

By Nothing Else

Than by merely
A single, all-powerful corrosive stain
That pours itself everywhere, dissolving
All greatness
And here is called TIME, man becomes
Blotches upon the furniture that possessed him.

Slowly digested
By the entrails of his dwelling place,
The slight warmth
Of a brief existence seeps
Into the stonework behind the wallpaper
Until he
Is no longer what he is but an
Indefinable odor of his house,
No longer imaginable:
That particular everyman.

On the Threshold

To sit on the threshold
Of the house in the dunes,
Seeing nothing
But sun, feeling nothing
But warmth, hearing nothing
But the surf and believing, now
Between two heart-
Beats, this
Is peace.

Film Put in Backwards

When I woke
I woke in the breathless black
Of the box.

Auf zu meinen Häupten. Erdschollen
Flogen flatternd zur Schaufel zurück.
Die teure Schachtel mit mir dem teuren
Verblichenen stieg schnell empor.
Der Deckel klappte hoch und ich
Erhob mich und fühlte gleich: Drei
Geschosse fuhren aus meiner Brust
In die Gewehre der Soldaten die
Abmarschierten schnappend
Aus der Luft ein Lied
Im ruhig festen Tritt
Rückwärts.

Sorgen

Der zu leben sich entschliesst
Muss wissen
Warum er gestern zur Nachtzeit erwachte
Wohin er heute durch die Strassen geht
Wozu er morgen in seinem Zimmer
Die Wände mit weissem Kalk anstreicht.

War da ein Schrei?
Ist da ein Ziel?
Wird da Sicherheit sein?

Das Fenster ist aufgestossen

Noch keine Helle am Himmel. Rauch in
Der Luft. Draussen auf dem Kies
Eine Gestalt.
Unkenntlich. Vermummt von Dunst und
Zwielicht.
Klopft an das schwarze, rissige Holz
Deiner Tür.

I heard: the earth
Was opening over me. Clods
Fluttered back
                    To the shovel. The
Dear box, with me the dear
                    Departed, gently rose.
The lid flew up and I
Stood, feeling:
                    Three bullets travel
Out of my chest
Into the rifles of soldiers, who
                    Marched off, gasping
Out of the air a song
With calm firm steps
                    Backwards.

Worries

He who decides to live
Must know why last night
He woke up, where
He is going today through the streets,
For what purpose he will whitewash
His room tomorrow.

Was there a scream?
Is there an aim?
Will the place be safe?

The Window Has Blown Open

Still no light in the sky. Smoke
In the air. Outside on the gravel
A figure.
Unrecognizable. Wrapped in mist
And twilight.
Knocks at the black, cracked wood
Of your door.

Und fragst du nach dem Namen jener, die
An dein Haus pocht, wird es leise sagen:

Die du aus deinem Leben gestossen
Wie unnützen Ballast.
Die du hast fortlaufen lassen
Wie schmutziges Spülwasser.
Die du hast verdorren lassen
Wie den Fliederbaum in der Hitze
Des Mittags.
Die immer stirbt. Die immer wiederkehrt.

Wahrheit heisse ich.
Nichts hält mich auf: Nicht das Holz
Deiner Tür. Nicht die Tür deines Zimmers.
Nicht die Haut deines Fleisches. Nicht
Das knöcherne Dach über deinem Hirn.
Ich komme hinein.

Wie die Morgenröte.
Wie der Tag, den nichts hindert
Am Kommen.

Zweifacher Monolog—kurzgeschlossen

O über unsere Kinder, die Computer,
o ihr ohnmächtiges Mitleid für uns:
mit zerstanzter Zunge reden sie
logisch und zwecklos, weil Logik, weil Zweck,
an Väter gewendet, o nur Verschwendung bedeutet:
unrationeller Irrationalismus
elektronenschneller stillgestandner Kuben,
von oben bis unten nichts als Gehirn,
das denkt und denkt
und denkt:
O über unsere Bediener, die Sauerstoffel
und Ach

And if you ask the name of whoever it is
Rapping on your house, a voice will say:

The one you drove out of your life
Like useless ballast.
The one you poured away
Like old dishwater.
Whom you allowed to go dry
Like the lilac in the heat
Of noonday.
Who is always dying. Always returning.

I am called truth.
Nothing stops me: not the wood
Of your door. Not the door of your room.
Not the skin of your flesh. Not
The bone roof over your brain.
I am coming in.

Like the sunrise.
Like the day which nothing can stop
From coming.

Twofold Monologue—Short-circuited

O for our offspring, the computers,
o their impotent compassion for us:
with perforated tongues they talk
logically and without purpose, for logic and purpose,
directed at fathers, is only extravagance:
unrationed irrationalism
of static cubes quick as electrons,
from top to toe nothing but brain
which thinks and thinks
and thinks:
O for our attendants, the oxyginks,
and alas

und Wehe den lymphatischen Gespenstern,
unfähig zu wahrer Logik, zu dem reinen Zweck:
O über unsere kindlichen Erzeuger: O O O O
O O O O O O O O O
OOOOOOOO
oooooo

Spekulationen des Gedichteschreibers
übers Gedichteschreiben

1
Damit ja nicht zufällig
das ewige Feuer unserer Vergänglichkeit
Augen professioneller Leser blende, dichten Dichter
verwendungslose Wandungen ihrer Werke
mit Bildungskitt, verknetet
zu zähem Geklump änigmatischen Dekors:
unterschlagene Fundsachen
aus allen literarischen waste lands.

2
Damit nicht
Wirklichkeit durchsickert, rötlich und
lymphatisch zumeist, übel riechend, sind
Gedichte aus Kunststoff
und hermetischer als unterirdische Bunkertüren,
geöffnet erst zum Verderben, Tresore Pandoras,
und undurchdringlicher
als das Gespinst der Spione, pensionsberechtigter
Spinnen, amtlicher Asseln, glamourösen
Gewürms, wimmelnd
unter der zerborstenen Gesetzesplatte.

3
Besser
den Samen zur Erde rinnen und den Ton
zerbröckeln lassen oder verklingen: Schweigen
wäre
eine messbare Frequenz nicht verlautbarter
lauterer Wahrheit.

and woe to the lymphatic ghosts,
incapable of true logic, of pure purpose:
O for our childish progenitors: O O O O
O O O O O O O O O
OOOOOOOO
oooooo

Speculations about the Writing of Poems,
by the Writer of Poems

1
Lest by some mishap
the eternal fire of our transience
blind professional readers' eyes, poets plug
the unusable hulks of their works
with cultural putty, kneaded into
tough lumps of enigmatic décor:
purloined *trouvailles*
from all the literary wastelands.

2
Lest
reality trickle through, reddish and
lymphatic mainly, malodorous, poems are
of artificial stuff
and more hermetic than bunker doors underground,
open only for ruin, Pandora's hoard,
and more impenetrable
than spy networks, the webs
of pensionable spiders, bug officialdom, glamorized
worms that seethe
under the broken paving of law.

3
Better
to let the seed spill on the earth and the tone
crumble or fade: silence
would be
a measurable frequency of undeclared
clear and loud truth.

4
Aber besser das immer Ungenügende:
schmucklos und knapp bemessenen Materials, Gefäss
einem Flämmchen, wenig
vom Umkreis erhellend, doch wenig ist mehr als nichts.
Das Rechte zu sagen, ist mehr
als das Richtige.
Die unentwegt Geschäftigen, fleissig an eigener
Hybris tätig, für die gute Unendlichkeit
einer Sekunde stören.
Von der Zukunft, dem dunklen Gebirge, wissen,
es führt
eine Pforte hinein in die Schatzkammer, wenn man

das Schlüsselwort ruft: Dieses eine
nennen mit allen anderen
ist besser als jedes beste.

Berliner Nachmittag

Im Sommer bei bedecktem Himmel
im Sommer bei sanftem Regen
im Sommer in der Kühle alter Wohnungen
zwischen dunkler Tapeten Gesichtsträchtigkeit:
da liegen
und auf die Stadtbahn lauschen
gedämpfter Schwellenstoss
Traben der Droschken
Stakkato handbetriebener Maschinen
in weggeblasenen Hinterhöfen
sterbliches Spiel verwehter Leiber
blass in der Blässe heimlicher Betten
versteckt hinter bröckelndem Stuck
hinter wucherndem Schorf alter Häuser
die eines plötzlichen Nachmittags
von Dumpern und Kränen samt Inhalt
unbekränzt überführt werden
aus ihrem Dasein in mein Erinnern

4
But the never enough is better:
of plain material, short in measure, vessel
for a small flame, illuminating
little of its world, yet little is more than nothing.
To say the right thing is more
than correctness.
To disturb for the good
infinity of a second those
perpetual busybodies laboring
at their own hubris.
To know of the future, that dark mountain,
that a door to the treasure opens, if

> one speaks the magic word: to speak this
> one word with all the others
> is better than every best thing.

Berlin Afternoon

In summer under a cloudy sky
in summer with a mild rain falling
in summer in the coolness of old rooms
in among old wallpapers freighted with visions:
to lie there
and listen to the trams
clunk of wheels over gaps in the rails
gallop of cabs
staccato of hand-driven machines
in blown-away back yards
mortal play of vanished bodies
pale in the pallor of secret beds
hidden behind crumbling stucco
behind the teeming scurf of old houses
which one sudden afternoon unwreathed
are carried away by dump trucks and cranes
complete with their contents
out of their existence into our memory

wo ihre begrüsste und beweinte Vergänglichkeit
zum Stillstand kommt: im Sommer
bei sanftem Regen.

Übersetzung eines deutschen Sprichwortes
in Historische Kinetik

Vorm Eintreten die Zunge reinigen!
Der Hausherr leidet an empfindsamen Ohren,
ungleich seinen Gästen, den zwangsläufigen,
die mehr am Gemüt (oder was sie so nennen).

Nicht Seiler erwähnen, nicht Sisal,
kein hanfnes Tabu, dessen Tage vergangen,
dessen Tage verkommen—gebeten wird trotzdem
und stürmisch gefordert:
Nicht davon sprechen, man spricht nicht
davon,
tut sowas nicht, weil man es nicht tut, ergo:
man sei man: Ideal, jedem erreichbar.

Die ihre Lippen ungenügend gehütet jedoch,
hängt der Unaussprechliche am Unausgesprochenen
auf.

Passbild eines Paradiesbürgers

Für Heinz von Cramer

Offenen Mundes braucht er nichts weiter
als eine neue Programmierung:
Füttert ihn mit daumenschmalem Gängelband
bestanzt mit dem kleinsten Einmaleins
das sich findet
das immer noch zu gewaltig für einen
der hungert und dürstet und sich potenziert

where their transience welcomed and wept for
stops: in summer
with a mild rain falling.

Translation of a German Proverb into
Historical Kinetics

Before you enter, clean your tongue!
The landlord suffers from sensitive ears,
unlike his lodgers, the obligatory ones,
whose trouble is feeling (or whatever they call it).

Don't mention rope makers, or sisal,
no hemp taboo, whose days are gone,
whose days perish—nevertheless you are asked
and tempestuously told:
Not to speak of it, one just doesn't speak
of it,
don't do it, because one simply doesn't, therefore:
one may be one: ideal, to all attainable.

But those who have not held their tongues enough
are hung
from that which is unspoken by the unspeakable one.

Passport Photograph of a Citizen of Paradise
                              for Heinz von Cramer

Open-mouthed he needs only
a new programming:
feed him with a halter thin as a thumb,
punched with the littlest one-times-one
to be found
which still is too strong for a man
who is hungry and thirsty and multiplies himself

und damit Hunger und Durst. Der
was er rechts vom Komma besitzt
die Vernunft substrahiert und sich stets
verrechnet
zählt er auf sich.

Der schreit
weil er die Sterne beziffert und
keine anderen Sorgen mehr hat
als den ihm innewohnenden
den ihm äusserlichen Leerelauf zu regulieren
dass am Ende die Rechnung aufgehe:
Minus plus Minus
gleich Plus.

Dieser summarisch lebenden Einzahl wegen
ward Gott
durch Wissenschaft volltransistorisiert.
Seinethalben
entdeckt mittels Philosophie und Druckerschwärze
eine neue Welt in der alten
wahrhaft vierte Dimension:
Herein ohne anzuklopfen.

Also frei und glücklich wie nie
fällt er täglich einen Baum der Erkenntnis
und ein Urteil
und rezitiert
nur ein kurzes Countdown eh es vollstreckt
an immer wieder sich
er selbst.

Vergesslichkeit

Jener römische Kaiser, der mit dem quadratischen Schnurrbart
und dem flotten Dreispitz auf der Perücke, der das Fett auffangen
liess, tropfend aus den brennenden Ketzern, um die Motore seiner
Bomber zu schmieren, der eisernen Adler, die seinen Legionen
voranflogen nach Gallien, nach Albion, nach Polen—wie denn
nur war sein wohlklingender jeweiliger Name?

with hunger and thirst. Who
subtracts the amount to the right
of the decimal point, that is, reason and
who always miscalculates when
he's counting on himself.

Who cries out
because he gives numbers to the stars and
has no other troubles
beyond the regulation of his interior
his exterior idling
to make the sum come out all right in the end:
minus plus minus
equals plus.

This summarily existent unit, for him
science has
fully transistorized God.
For his sake
a new world discovers in the old
via philosophy and printer's ink
the veritable fourth dimension:
Enter without knocking.

Thus free and happy as never before
he fells each day a tree of knowledge,
passing judgment,
and recites
only a short countdown before it
is he himself whom over and over
he executes.

Forgetfulness

That Roman emperor, the one with the oblong moustache and
the smart three-cornered hat on his wig, who had the fat which
dripped from heretics caught to grease his bombers' engines, the
iron eagles that preceded his legions into Gaul, Albion, Poland—
just what was it now, the fine-sounding name he had?

Die Schreie der Fledermäuse

Während sie in der Dämmerung durch die Luft schnellen, hierhin, dorthin, schreien sie laut, aber ihr Schreien wird nur von ihresgleichen gehört. Baumkronen und Scheunen, verfallende Kirchentürme werfen ein Echo zurück, das sie im Fluge vernehmen und das ihnen meldet, was sich an Hindernissen vor ihnen erhebt und wo ein freier Weg ist. Nimmt man ihnen die Stimme, finden sie keinen Weg mehr; überall anstossend und gegen Wände fahrend, fallen sie tot zu Boden. Ohne sie nimmt, was sonst sie vertilgen, überhand und grossen Aufschwung: das Ungeziefer.

Schatten entziffern

Wer zu lesen verstünde
die Buchstaben die keine sind:
bemooster Ziegel vom Dach
brandiges Holz noch vom Krieg
Blöcke geborstnen Betons

und die Schatten am Morgen
korrigiert von den Schatten des Abends
in den Häuserzeilen
zwischen denen
alle Wahrheiten stehen.

Regen

In der Welt der zerstörten Bilder,
der unglaubhaften Schriften
bezeichnet der Regen die Fassaden
mit Eindeutigkeit:

Schau meine Werke, feucht und
fröhlich: Fäulnis
verbreitend, die Leben ist.

The Shrieking of Bats

While they whizz through the air in the twilight, hither and thither, they shriek out loud, but their shrieks are heard only by their own kind. Treetops and barns, decrepit steeples throw back an echo which they hear in their flight and which tells them what obstacles are looming in front and when the way is open. If you deprive them of their voices, they cannot find the way anymore; everywhere colliding with things and flying against walls, they fall dead to the ground. Without them there is an overwhelming increase of what they normally destroy: vermin.

To Decipher Shadows

If somebody knew how to read
those letters that are not letters:
moss-covered tile from the roof
timber charred in the last war
blocks of burst concrete

and the morning shadows
corrected by evening shadows
in terrace rows
between which
all truths are recorded.

Rain

In the world of broken images
of implausible scripts
the rain covers house fronts
with unambiguous signs:

Look at my works, damp and
cheerful: spreading
decay that is life.

Aqua destillata gebiert
nichts: Reinheit
ist fruchtlos.

Studiere den Regen: jeder Tropfen
ist wahr.

Tagebuchnotiz

Geträumt gen Morgen hin,
Gespenst zu sein: ein Spuk
in Windsor Castle
im Angesicht der Königin:
unbegreifliches Ding
vor ihren ungreifbaren Brüsten.
Handloses Wehen: ich
und nichts weiter als Traum
eines Traumes.

Mündliche Verlautbarung

Das ganze Problem ist
da es das eine der Welt
ist es unwirklich und einfach zugleich
wie der Traum:
den Fuss in die stählerne Weiche geklemmt
den Zug auf sich zufahren sehen.

Mit der Lokomotive wurde geredet:
ihr eigen ist volles Verständnis
aber kann selber nicht einhalten.
Ein ernsthaftes Wort gesprochen auch
mit der Schiene die aus eigenem Antrieb
keinesfalls
den Fuss festhält.

Distilled water gives birth to
nothing: Purity
is infertile.

Study the rain: every drop
is true.

Diary Entry

Dreamed toward morning
That I was a spook, haunting
Windsor Castle
in the Queen's presence:
incomprehensible thing
in front of untouchable breasts.
A handless wafting: I
and no more than the dream
of a dream.

Oral Declaration

The whole problem is
since it's the only one
it's unreal and simple at once
like dreams:
one foot wedged into the steel points
to see the train come at you.

The engine was open to talk:
its nature is full understanding
but it can't choose to stop.
Serious words, too, were exchanged
with the rail which on its own initiative
never
will trap a foot.

Wir alle sind uns einig darüber
dass unsere Lage aussichtslos ist.

Ja besser
es wäre vorher kein Kessel angeheizt worden.
Ja besser ungestellt die Weichen.
Ja nimmermehr begangen
wäre besser geblieben
die alte Strecke.

Antwort an Pilatus auf seine Frage

Es ist
das fast Glaubhafte,
ausgehöhlt von fressenden Sekunden,
brüchig,
von jedem Windhauch gefährdet,
mühsam gestützt
vom feilen Adjektiv.

We all agree about one thing
that our situation is hopeless

True, better
the boiler had never been stoked.
True, better the points had been switched.
True, never to have taken
the old railway track
would have been better.

Reply to Pilate's Question

It is
the almost plausible,
hollowed out by devouring seconds,
fragile,
imperilled by every breeze,
laboriously propped up
by the venal adjective.

Heinz Kahlau
(b. 1931)

Der alte Maurer

Johannes, der alte Maurer, ist tot.
Wie der Mörtel,
mit dem er Stein zu Steinen fügte,
ist sein Gesicht.
Seine Hände auch.

Der Junge,
den er gestern schelten musste—
wegen Achtlosigkeit—
bekam seine Kelle.

Vom Schornstein,
der sein letzter wurde,
stieg heute morgen
der erste Rauch.

Begrabt ihn ohne Lügen.

Zeitungen

Am Morgen stand in der Zeitung:
Ein Mann wurde verurteilt.
Für wen und gegen wen?
Wer sprach das Urteil?
Für wen und gegen wen?
In der Zeitung stand nur:
Der Mann wurde verurteilt.
Wem gehörte die Zeitung—
und wem der Mann?

Genesung

Nun
gehöre ich wieder
zu euch.
Meine Hände bluten wieder.
Wenn ich jetzt

The Old Bricklayer*

John, the old bricklayer, is dead.
Like the cement
with which he joined brick to brick
is his face now.
His hands too.

The boy
whom yesterday he had to reprimand—
for carelessness—
inherited his trowel.

From the chimney
that was his last
this morning the first
smoke rose up.

Bury him without lies.

Newspapers

This morning we read in the newspaper:
A man was convicted.
For whom and against whom?
Who pronounced the verdict?
For whom and against whom?
The newspaper only reported:
The man was convicted.
Who owned the newspaper—
and who owned the man?

Recovery

Now once more
I'm part
of you all.
My hands bleed again.
When now

unter euch bin,
fürchte ich nicht nur
um alle.

Nun
fürchte ich wieder
um mich.

I'm with you
I don't only fear
for everyone.

Now once more
I fear
for myself.

Reiner Kunze
(b. 1933)

Der Hochwald erzieht seine Bäume

Der hochwald erzieht seine bäume

Sie des lichtes entwöhnend, zwingt er sie,
all ihr grün in die kronen zu schicken
Die fähigkeit,
mit allen zweigen zu atmen,
das talent,
äste zu haben nur so aus freude,
verkümmern

Den regen siebt er, vorbeugend
der leidenschaft des durstes

Er lässt die bäume grösser werden
wipfel an wipfel:
Keiner sieht mehr als der andere,
dem wind sagen alle das gleiche

Holz

Die Bringer Beethovens

für Ludvik Kundera

Sie zogen aus, Beethoven zu bringen
jedermann
Und da sie auch eine schallplatte hatten
spielten sie zur rascheren einsicht
die sinfonie nr. 5 c-moll opus 67

Der mensch M. aber sagte,
es sei ihm zu laut, das
mache sein alter

Über nacht setzten die bringer Beethovens
maste an strassen und plätze
spannten drähte befestigten

The Timber Forest Educates its Trees

The timber forest educates its trees

By weaning them from light compels them
to send all their green into their tops
The ability
to breathe with every bough,
the talent
of having branches for the sheer joy of it
are stunted

The forest filters rain, as a precaution
against the passion of thirst

Lets the trees grow taller
crest to crest:
None sees more than another,
to the wind each one of them says

Wood

The Bringers of Beethoven

For Ludvik Kundera

They set out to bring Beethoven
to everyone.
And as they had a record with them
they played for speedier understanding
Symphony no. 5, in C minor, opus 67

But the man M. said
it was too loud for him, he
was getting old

In the night the bringers of Beethoven put
up poles in streets and squares
hooked up cables, connected

lautsprecher und mit dem morgen
ertönte zur bessren gewöhnung
die sinfonie nr. 5 c-moll opus 67,
laut genug dass sie gehört ward
auch in der ferne

Der mensch M. aber sagte, ihn schmerze der kopf,
ging heim gegen mittag schloss
türen und fenster und lobte
die dicke der mauern

Herausgefordert, knüpften die bringer Beethovens
draht an die mauern und hingen
lautsprecher über die fenster dass
durch die scheiben drang
die sinfonie nr. 5 c-moll opus 67

Der mensch M. aber ging aus dem haus und zeigte an
die bringer Beethovens;
doch jeder fragte ihn, was er habe
gegen Beethoven

Angegriffen, klopften die bringer Beethovens
am tore des menschen M., stellten als er es auftat
hinter die schwelle den fuss; die sauberkeit lobend
traten sie ein
Zufällig kam auch die rede
auf Beethoven
und zur belebung des themas hatten sie
zufällig bei sich
die sinfonie nr. 5 c-moll opus 67

Der mensch M. aber schlug mit der eisernen schöpfkelle
ein auf die bringer Beethovens
Er wurde verhaftet zur zeit

Mörderisch nannten die tat des M.
anwalt und richter der bringer Beethovens
Doch hoffnung sei immer
Er wurde verurteilt

loudspeakers, and with the dawn
for more thorough acquaintance came the strains of
Symphony no. 5, in C minor, opus 67,
came loud enough to be heard
in the mute fields.

But the man M. said he had a headache,
went home about noon, closed
doors and windows and praised
the thickness of the walls

Thus provoked, the bringers of Beethoven strung
wire on to the walls and hung
loudspeakers over the windows, and in
through the panes came
Symphony no. 5, in C minor, opus 67

But the man M. stepped out of the house and denounced
the bringers of Beethoven;
they all asked him what he had
against Beethoven

Thus attacked, the bringers of Beethoven knocked
on M.'s door and when they opened up they
forced a foot inside; praising the neatness of the place
they went in.
The conversation happened to turn
to Beethoven,
and to enliven the subject they happened
to have with them
Symphony no. 5, in C minor, opus 67

But the man M. hit the bringers of
Beethoven with an iron ladle.
He was arrested just in time.

M.'s act was called homicidal
by lawyers and judges of the bringers of Beethoven.
But they must not give up hoping.
He was sentenced

zur sinfonie nr. 5 c-moll opus 67
von Ludwig van Beethoven

Da trommelte M. und schrie
bis stille war

Er war schon zu alt, sagten die bringer Beethovens
Am sarge des M. aber, sagten sie,
stehn seine kinder

Und die kinder verfügten
dass gespielt werde
am sarge des menschen M.
die sinfonie nr. 5 c-moll opus 67

Das Ende der Fabeln

Es war einmal ein fuchs . . .
beginnt der hahn
eine fabel zu dichten

Da merkt er
so geht's nicht
denn hört der fuchs die fabel
wird er ihn holen

Es war einmal ein bauer . . .
beginnt der hahn
eine fabel zu dichten

Da merkt er
so geht's nicht
denn hört der bauer die fabel
wird er ihn schlachten

Es war einmal . . .

Schau hin schau her
Nun gibt's keine fabeln mehr

to Symphony no. 5, in C minor, opus 67,
by Ludwig van Beethoven

M. kicked and screamed,
until the loudspeakers stopped
beyond the mute fields

He was just too old, the bringers of Beethoven said.
But by M.'s coffin, they said,
are his children

And his children demanded
that over the coffin of
the man M. should be played
Symphony no. 5, in C minor, opus 67

The End of Fables

Once upon a time there was a fox . . .
the rooster begins
to make up a fable

But realizes
it can't be done like that
for if the fox hears the fable
he'll come and get him

Once upon a time there was a farmer . . .
the rooster begins
to make up a fable

But realizes
it can't be done like that
for if the farmer hears the fable
he'll wring his neck

Once upon a time . . .

Look for them here look for them there
You'll find no fables anywhere

Das Ende der Kunst

Du darfst nicht, sagte die eule zum auerhahn,
du darfst nicht die sonne besingen
Die sonne ist nicht wichtig

Der auerhahn nahm
die sonne aus seinem gedicht

Du bist ein künstler,
sagte die eule zum auerhahn

Und es war schön finster

Kurzer Lehrgang

DIALEKTIK

Unwissende damit ihr
unwissend bleibt

werden wir euch
schulen

AESTHETIK

Bis zur entmachtung des
imperialismus ist
als verbündet zu betrachten

Picasso

ETHIK

Im mittelpunkt steht
der mensch

Nicht
der einzelne

The End of Art

You must not, said the owl to the capercailzie,
you must not sing of the sun
The sun is not important

The capercailzie took
the sun out of its poem

You are an artist,
said the owl to the capercailzie

And all was dark

Brief Curriculum

DIALECTICS

Ignorant people so that
you'll remain ignorant

we shall
school you

AESTHETICS

Until imperialism has
been defeated
regard as an ally

Picasso

ETHICS

In the center stands
mankind

Not
this man or that man

Von der Notwendigkeit der Zensur

Retuschierbar ist
alles

Nur
das negativ nicht
in uns

Jeder Tag

für Elisabeth

Jeder tag
ist ein brief

Jeden abend
versiegeln wir ihn

Die nacht
trägt ihn fort

Wer
empfängt ihn

Dorf in Mähren

für Peter Huchel

Fünf jahre heiratete niemand
in Toubor keiner
starb kein kind
wurde geboren

Lautlos blüht am hang
die wegwarte

The Need for Censorship

Everything
can be retouched

except
the negative
inside us

Every Day

                              for Elisabeth

Every day
is a letter

Every evening
we seal it

The night
carries it off

Who
receives it

Village in Moravia

                              for Peter Huchel

For five years no one married
in Toubǒr no one
died no child
was born

Silently on the slope
the chicory flowers

Düsseldorfer Impromptu

Der himmel zieht die erde an
wie geld geld

Bäume aus
glas und stahl, morgens
voll glühender früchte

Der mensch
ist dem menschen
ein ellenbogen

Fanfare für Vietnam

Meine worte will ich schicken gegen
bomber
          bomber
                    bomber

Mit meinen worten will ich auffangen
bomben
          bomben
                    bomben

Meine worte aber haben
                                        handschellen

*Einundzwanzig Variationen
über das Thema „die Post"*

I
Wenn die post
hinters fenster fährt blühn
die eisblumen gelb

Düsseldorf Impromptu

The sky attracts the earth
as money attracts money

trees
of glass and steel, each morning
laden with glowing fruit

Man
to man is
an elbow

Fanfare for Vietnam

My words I will send out against
bombers
          bombers
                    bombers

With my words I will stop the fall of
bombs
        bombs
              bombs

My words however are
                            handcuffed

*Twenty-one Variations
on the Theme "The Mail"*

I
When the mail van
pulls up behind the window
the iceferns put out
yellow flowers

2
Brief du
zweimillimeteröffnung
der tür zur welt du
geöffnete öffnung du
lichtschein,
durchleuchtet, du

bist angekommen

3
Tochter, briefträgerin vom
briefkasten bis zum
tisch, deine stimme ist
das posthorn

4
O aus
einem fremden land, sieh
die marken . . . Wie
heisst das land?

— — —

Deutschland, tochter

5
O ist
die marke schön: der wolf und
die sieben geisslein und
seine pfote ist
ganz weiss . . . Wer
hat den brief geschrieben?

Vielleicht
die sieben geisslein,
vielleicht
der wolf

2
Letter you
two millimeter opening
of the door to the world you
opened opening you
chink of light,
translucent, you

have arrived

3
Daughter, carrier of
mail from mailbox to
table, your voice is
the post horn

4
O from
a foreign country, look,
the stamps . . . What
is the country called?

— — —

Germany, daughter

5
How lovely
the stamp is: the wolf and
the seven kids and
his paw is
pure white . . . Who
wrote the letter?

May-be
the seven kids.
May-be
the wolf

. . . der wolf ist tot!

Im märchen, tochter, nur
im märchen

6
Tochter
du plünderst kuverts? Ach nur
das blaue schiff und
den lustigen hahn?
Die stempel sind lesbar:
HAMBURG PARIS

Ich will alle briefmarken
wegschliessen

7
Tochter—
briefmarkensammeln was
ist das schon

Wie ein schmetterling
leicht werden wenn
du eine schmetterlingsmarke siehst

wie ein vogel
fortfliegen wenn
du eine vogelmarke siehst

8
O freude des frankierens

Der brief ist
ein weisser hals
die marke
das amulett

. . . the wolf is dead!

In the fairy tale, daughter, only
in the fairy tale

6
Daughter
you're plundering envelopes? Ah, only
the blue boat and
the merry rooster?
The postmarks are legible:
HAMBURG PARIS

I'd better lock up
all the stamps

7
Daughter—
stamp collecting, what
does it amount to

Becoming light as
a butterfly when
you see a butterfly stamp

flying away like
a bird when
you see a bird stamp

8
O the joy of stamping mail

The letter is
a white neck
the stamp
an amulet

der brief ist
eine wolke
die marken
sind vögel

der brief ist
schnee
die marken
sind mäuse

der brief ist
das tischtuch
die marken
sind rosen

(schalterbeamte ihr
entwertet ein
kunstwerk)

9
HIER BEDIENT
POSTHAUPTASSISTENTIN L.

Hinter der barriere,
auf die ich meine nackten briefe lege,
sitzen
Sie

Sie verfügen
über feuersalamander auf rotem gestein
über scharen kleiner igel
über schmetterlinge in orange und hellblau

Sie
sind gott

Sie verpassen meinen briefen
grasgrüne uniformen

Sie
sind der feldwebel

the letter is
a cloud
the stamps
are birds

the letter is
snow
the stamps
are mice

the letter is
the tablecloth
the stamps
are roses

(post office clerks
you deface
a work of art)

9
THIS POSITION IS
SERVED BY HEAD ASSISTANT MISS L.

Behind the counter
on which I lay my bare letter
you sit

you dispose
of salamanders on red scree
of bevies of baby hedgehogs
of butterflies in orange and pale blue

you
are God

you issue to my letters
grass-green uniforms

you
are the sergeant-major

10

Niemals beschwere dich über
die post

An allen schaltern
verweigert sie dir

die kleinste
billigste die
letzte
der verweigerbaren freuden—

die
seltene
gewöhnliche
zwanziger

11
Brief
du fliegst die grenze an

Ich wünsche dir
einen himmel aus papier,
die grössere geschwindigkeit

Du
trägst keine bomben

12

    Eilzustellung / Exprès
    Berlin (west) 20.1.–13 uhr
    Greiz   26.1.–21 uhr

    Brief
    Berlin (west) 1.2.–17 uhr
    Greiz   9.2.

Was
der tochter sagen im
postmuseum?

10
Never complain about
the mail

At every counter
it refuses you

the smallest
cheapest the
least of
refusable pleasures—

the
rare
ordinary
twenty stamp

11
Letter
you fly against the frontier

I wish you
a sky made of paper,
and greater speed

you
carry no bombs

12
      Special delivery / Express
      Berlin (West) 20 Jan.—13 hours
      Greiz   26 Jan.—21 hours

      Letter
      Berlin (West) 1 Feb.—17 hours
      Greiz   9 Feb.

What
am I to tell my daughter
in the post museum?

13
Tochter, schwer
fällt das warten bis
der zug kommt bis
er abfährt bis
wir aussteigen

Doch wenn man stirbt
zwischen zwei briefen

14
Schöne weiber
kursierten unter den belagerern
Neapels, hinsank
das heer an
syphilis

Alle nachrichten sind
weiber

15
Bad Godesberg, 4.9.
„. . . wir haben die Nachforschungen nach
dem letzten Einschreibebrief bei der Post
eingeleitet: bisher noch ohne Ergebnis . . .“

Bad Godesberg, 10.9.
„. . . vielen Dank für Ihren letzten Brief, dem
ich entnehmen muss, dass Sie auch mein letztes
Schreiben nicht erhalten haben . . .“

Bonn, 26.10.
„Zu dieser Postsache: Sie landete wohl dort,
wo wir vermuteten, denn wir erhielten die
Bestätigung. Der Brief wurde an Sie nicht

13
Daughter, it's hard
to wait for the train
to arrive for the train to
leave for us
to open the door

But what if one dies
between two letters

14
Beautiful women
circulated among the besiegers
of Naples, the army
went down with
syphilis

all messages are
women

15
Bad Godesberg, 4 Sept.
". . . we have initiated enquiries for the last
registered letter: with no results to date . . ."

Bad Godesberg, 10 Sept.
". . . many thanks for your last letter from which
I regret to learn that you failed to receive my last
communication also . . ."

Bonn, 26 Oct.
"Concerning that item of mail, it must have
arrived where we assumed it had arrived, for
we received confirmation. The letter was not

weitergeleitet . . . Übrigens war darin noch
ein Brief eines Mannes aus der Schweiz an
Sie . . ."

Briefe ihr
weissen läuse im
pelz des vaterlands, wartet,
die post ist
ein kamm!

16

für Jan Skácel

Briefträger, freunde, wenn
mir's nicht mehr reichen wird für
briefmarken, gebt mir

eine mütze
eine tasche
eine strasse und
viel post

Ich werde
keinen brief verlieren, die ecken
nicht umknicken (VORSICHT
BEI DEN GROSSEN ANSICHTSKARTEN—ich
weiss)

Trauerschreiben
halte ich zurück bis
alle briefe ausgetragen sind

Stets
trag ich mit mir einen brief für
entmutigte

(Nur überlasst mir keinen brief aus
Mähren, ich
begänne zu dichten)

forwarded to you . . . In addition, you may be
interested to know, it contained another letter to
you from a man in Switzerland . . ."

Letters you
white lice in
the fatherland's pelt, wait,
the mail is
a comb!

16
                                        for Jan Skácel

Postmen, friends, when
I can no longer afford
stamps, give me

a cap
a bag
a street and
lots of mail

I shan't lose
a single letter, nor bend
the corners (TAKE CARE
WITH LARGE PICTURE POSTCARDS—I
know)

Letters with black edges
I shall withhold until
all the others have been delivered

Always
I shall carry a letter for
discouraged people

(Only don't entrust me with a letter
from Moravia, or
I'd start writing poems)

17
Briefträger sein

Tag für tag
erwartet werden, eine
hoffnung sein, das unüberbrückbare
überbrücken mit
jedem schritt

Briefträger sein

Tag für tag
bis vor die türen der menschen gehen, nicht
eintreten dürfen

In diesen zeiten

18
Es läutet—um
diese zeit?

Die
eilpost! Die welt
gibt ein zeichen!

— — —

GUTEN TAG WIR
HÄTTEN UNS GERN MIT IHNEN
UNTERHALTEN . . .

19
Wie ein gitter
fällt der schatten der fensterstäbe
aufs papier.

Es ist weiss.

Schuld genug.

17
To be a postman

Be expected
day after day, be a
hope, to bridge the
unbridgeable with
every step

To be a postman

Day after day
go as far as the doors of people, not
be allowed to enter

In times like ours

18
There's a ring—at
this time of day!

Special
delivery! The world
is giving a sign!

— — —

GOOD MORNING WE
SHOULD LIKE A LITTLE
TALK WITH YOU . . .

19
Like a grille
the window-frame's shadow falls
on the paper.

It is white.

Guilt enough.

20
(unserer briefträgerin der
vielgeschmähten: IST DAS ALLES?!)

Einmal,
nach einem sehr schönen brief,
werde ich ein fest geben für
briefträger, die briefe austragen
aus leidenschaft, für
schalterbeamte, die grasgrüne marken
zum blühen bringen, ein
fest von
hier
bis
zum
briefkasten

21
Eines morgens
wird er läuten als
briefträger verkleidet

Ich werde ihn
durchschauen

Ich werde sagen: warte bis
der briefträger vorüber ist

20
(our postwoman's the
much maligned: IS THAT ALL?!)

One day,
after a very fine letter,
I shall throw a party
for postmen, postwomen who
deliver mail out of dedication, for
post office clerks who make
grass-green stamps flower, a
party from
here
to
the
mailbox

21
One morning
he will ring disguised
as a postman

I shall see
through his disguise

I shall say: wait
till the postman has come and gone

Nach der Geschichtsstunde

Die damals, der
Tamerlan war der
grausam: zehntausende seiner gefangenen liess er
binden an pfähle, mit mörtel und lehm
übergiessen lebendig
vermauern.

Tochter, die teilweise ausgrabung
jüngster fundamente
wird bereits
bereut

Zimmerlautstärke

Dann die
zwölf jahre
durfte ich nicht publizieren sagt
der mann im radio

Ich denke an X
und beginne zu zählen

Blickpunkt

Frau nicht
die möbel verrücken

Wer
im kopf umräumt dessen
schreibtisch muss

feststehn

After the History Lesson

Those people long ago, that
Tamerlaine, how
cruel they were: he had ten thousand of his prisoners
tied to posts, covered with mortar
and clay, immured
alive

Daughter, already
they're regretting the
partial excavation of
the latest foundations

Low Volume

Then for
twelve years
I was forbidden to publish
says the man on the radio

I think of X
and start counting

Perspective

No, don't
shift the furniture, dear

The man who
moves things around in his head
his desk must

stay put

Entschuldigung

Ding ist ding
sich selbst genug

Überflüssig
das zeichen

Überflüssig
das wort

(Überflüssig
ich)

Apology

A thing's a thing
sufficient to itself

Superfluous
the sign

Superfluous
the word

(Superfluous
I)

Sarah Kirsch
(b. 1935)

Januar

Ich bringe dir einen feuchten Fisch
einen schöngebauchten Flaschenfisch komm
wir tauschen Liebes zu dritt betreiben
ein gründliches Trinken

Eis schmilzt vom Fenster oder schmilzt nicht
die Dattelkerne
durchsprossen mit Blatt und Schaft das Papier
aus der Asche vom Teller
stülpen lila Blüten: jetzt

gehn wir ins Bild besteigen das Schiff

liegen auf harten grossmaschigen Netzen
fahren dem Mond den Nabel
dem Himmel ins Kreuz lachen
ob der verdatterten Dichter in Deutschland

liegen auf Ausschau im Bauch des Fisches

Die Kettenblüme Löwenzahn

Die Kettenblüme Löwenzahn trifft mich wo ich bin Deutsch-
lands Bahndämme staubige Winkel Äcker bewuchert sie noch
gestutzte Gärten nimmt sie durch Zäune die Blätter feine
Sägen Blüten jeden Tag neu sie hat den Wind er trägt über
Flüsse gemauerte Grenzen verklebt meine Finger wenn ich
gegen sie angehen will

eine zähe Begleiterin erst eine fröhliche Blume Spielzeug
Kranz der den Kopf spüren lässt Enttäuschung wenn sich die
Blüten im Zimmer nicht öffnen.

später der Ettersberg voller Löwenzahn idiotischer Frohsinn
aus Fundamenten von Häftlingsbaracken spritzt es hervor
gelbe Punkte Warnung vor Gas säumen Stufen zum Krema-
torium Kettenblumen Kinderblumen schönes Gelb Farbe
des Sommers

January

I bring you a damp fish
a fine-bellied bottle-fish come
we'll exchange loving among us three do
some heavy drinking

ice is melting on the window or perhaps is not
the date stones
pierce the paper with leaves and stem
mauve flowers open
out of the ash on the plate: now

we enter the picture board the ship

lie on hard broad-meshed nets
steer the navel of the moon
into the rear of the sky laugh
at the flabbergasted poets in Germany

lie on watch in the fish's belly

Dandelions for Chains

Dandelions meet me wherever I am they overrun Germany's
railway embankments dusty corners fields seize even well-
trimmed gardens through hedges leaves like fine saws new
flowers every day have the wind to carry them over rivers
walled boundaries stick my fingers together when I try to
fend them off

a tough companion first of all a gay flower plaything wreath
that makes you aware of your head disappointment when its
flowers won't open indoors

then Ettersberg covered with dandelions crazy joy yellow
spots shooting up from prison-camp foundations gas warning
line the steps to the crematorium flowers for chains flowers
for children beautiful yellow color of summer

reicht über den siebzehnten Breitengrad da wachsen kopf-
grosse Urwaldblumen hervor

Bevor die Sonne aufgeht

Bevor die Sonne aufgeht rufen meine Brüder die scheckigen
Hunde im Hof blasen die Hände schütteln Tau vom Schuh
eh die Sonne oben ist sind meine Brüder hinter dem Dorf
haben Netze ins Strauchwerk getan knüpfen einen Vogel fest
der ist geblendet und singt bis ans Ende die Brüder stopfen
sich Pfeifen liegen im Kraut sind geduldig folgen den kunst-
vollen Strophen jetzt hängen sieben im Netz sagt der Jüngste
und schneidet sich Schinken

Aber wenn der Vollmond hinter Wolken steht gehn meine
Brüder im Wald mit den Hunden biegen einander die Zweige
zurück sehn in den Himmel eine zersprungne Emaille-
schüssel sie legen dem Hickorybaum ihre Hände an rupfen
ein Gras blasen Hirsche hervor und treffen wie sies lernten
beim ersten Schuss kommen ächzend durch den Hof auf dem
Rücken brettsteife Last

Meine Brüder haben einen gelben Rock Sterne weiche faltige
Stiefel sie tragen einen Tornister es ist ein Bild von unserem
Haus darin verpackt eine Büchse Fleisch und ihr Vogelnetz
sie haben die neusten Gewehre gehn ausser Lands sie sollen
schiessen wenn ein Mensch im Visier ist ich kenne meine
Brüder sie biegen einander Zweige zurück und sind geduldig
bis ans Ende

extends across the seventeenth parallel where head-sized
jungle flowers bloom

Before the Sun Rises

Before the sun rises my brothers call the spotted dogs in the
yard blow their hands shake dew from their shoes before the
sun is up my brothers are behind the village have laid nets
in the undergrowth bind a bird up tightly it is blinded it sings
right to the end the brothers fill their pipes lie in the weeds
are patient follow the exquisite melodies there are seven
hanging in the net now says the youngest and cuts himself
some ham

But when the full moon is behind clouds my brothers walk in
the woods with the dogs hold the branches back for each other
see a cracked enamel pot in the sky they lay their hands on the
hickory tree pluck a blade of grass blow deer out into the
open and hit them as they learned to with the first shot come
groaning through the yard with a load as stiff as a board on
their backs

My brothers have got yellow greatcoats stars soft creased
boots they carry knapsacks there is a picture of our house
packed inside a tin of meat and their bird net they have the
latest guns go abroad they are to shoot when there is a man
in the sights I know my brothers they hold the branches back
for each other and are patient right to the end

Karl Mickel
(b. 1935)

Korrektes Haar

Ich brauche immer lange, eh ich anbeiss
Bei dir besonders. Liegts am Haar, das so
Verflucht korrekt ist, keine Strähne selbständig
Dass ich vermut, du schläfst bewegungslos?

Auch wird mir deine Freundlichkeit jetzt unheimlich
Das kann nicht gutgehn auf die Dauer, denk ich
Und steigre meinerseits die Komplimente derart
Dass Unernst vorherrscht und Routine aufkommt

Und das ist falsch. Denn wenns an deinem Haar liegt
Das du dir ordnest mit Routine, brauchts
Den derben Griff, der plötzlich planlos zugreift:
Nicht nach dem Haar, das löst sich dann von selber.

So weit der Plan. Berechnendes berechnen:
Ich denk nicht gern dran, aber leider oft.

Lamento und Gelächter

1
Und eine solche Traurigkeit ergriff mich des Abends
Dass ich zu den Leuten ging und ihnen klagte:
Ich gehöre zu den Toten des nächsten Kriegs!
Ich schreie zu euch: Helft mir, sonst scheide ich ab.
Also sprachen die Leute zu mir: Wer bist du
Dass wir dir helfen, was gehst du uns an, wem nützt du
Was hast du getan bislang? Und fragten sich untereinander:
Was will dieser Mensch von uns? wir kennen seiner nicht.
Wehe, sagte ich ihnen, ich sterbe, es kommt, es kommt
Bleckt herauf über mich. Wahrlich, ich sage euch:
Ich gehöre zu den Toten des nächsten Kriegs.
Und sie sprachen untereinander: Dieser Mann ist wahnsinnig.
Ausserdem haben wir Freizeit. So fahre er denn ab.

The Well-groomed Head

It takes some time before I take the bait
With you especially. Is it your hair
It's so damned neat, not one strand out of place
That I suspect you sleep quite motionless

Uncanny to me too is your good nature
In the long run. I think, this can't go well
And reinforce my stream of compliments
Until frivolity reigns, routine sets in

And that is wrong. For if it were your hair
And its routine arrangement I should need
Just one rough grab, the sudden planless lunge:
Not at your hair, that would unloose itself

So that's the plan. To calculate the calculable:
I don't like thinking of it, but alas I often do.

Lament and Laughter

I

Such sadness came over me in the evening
That I went to look for people and complained to them:
I am one of the dead of the next war!
I cry out to you: Help or I shall be gone.
Then those people said to me: Who are you
To deserve our help, what business of ours are you, to whom are
    you useful,
What have you done up to now? And they asked one another:
What does he want from us? We don't know him.
Oh, I said to them, I am dying, it's coming, it's coming,
It makes for me baring its teeth. Truly I tell you:
I am one of the dead of the next war.
And they said to one another: this man is mad.
Besides, we've finished work for the day. So he may as well go.

Und zum dritten Male hob ich an und bat sie
Flehend um Hilfe. Da legten sie sich schweigend in die Betten.
Und so bricht es herein über uns, sehet, es kommt, es kommt:
Herr, dein Wille geschehe. Ihr habt
Missachtet den geringsten eurer Brüder.
Ich gehöre zu den Toten des nächsten Kriegs.

2

Da aber lachte es schallend und lachte, erschallte
Gelächter aus tausenden Mündern, erhob sich zur Höhe
Der kreisenden Wolken des tödlichen Staubes, durchschnitt sie
Scharf wie die Sichel des Monds. Es lachte so plötzlich
Wie wenn eine Bombe zerplatzte, ein seltsames Lachen.
Niemals noch hatte ich früher so ein Lachen gehört.
Da fragte ich, etwas befremdet, die Leute: Was lacht ihr
Was habt ihr für Gründe zu lachen, alle auf ein Mal?
Merkst du nicht, sagten sie lachend, dass dieses Lachen
Das unsre Körper erschüttert, die Brustkästen weitet, die Lippen
Bis zum Zerspringen durchfährt, dass dieses Lachen
Nun deine Klagen hinweglacht, dass es die Grenzen des Datums
Ausbeult, hinausdrängt, zertrümmert? Was aber habt ihr
Beharrte ich, schon aus den Schuhen geschüttelt, was habt ihr
Für Gründe zu lachen, ich seh euch noch immer
Schwitzend die Arbeiten ausführn, seh euch des Abends
Müd über Büchern. Seht, eure Lider sind schwarz, eure Nächte
Sind euch entschieden zu kurz, die Mühsal der Tage
Die Drohung des Todes: habt ihr sie lachend vergessen?
Da war mir, als käme das Lachen nicht aus den Hälsen der Leute
Als wäre ihr Dasein Gelächter, als könnte keiner von ihnen
Wenn er gleich wollte, aufhörn. Ich lachte mich tot.

And for the third time I began and implored them
To help me. Then they lay down on their beds in silence.
And so it closes in on us, look, it's coming, it's coming:
Lord, thy will be done. You people
Have spurned the least of your brethren.
I am one of the dead of the next war.

2

But then somebody laughed, resounding, and laughter resounded
Out of a thousand mouths, rose up to the height
Of the circling clouds of deadly dust, cutting through them
Sharp as a sickle moon. It laughed all at once
As though a bomb were exploding, a strange kind of laughter.
Never before had I heard such laughter.
Then, a little perplexed, I asked those people: Why do you laugh
What reason have you to laugh, all at the same time?
Can't you see, they said laughing, that this laughter
Which shakes our bodies, expands our chests, twitches through
Our lips till they nearly burst, that this laughter
Now laughs your complaints away, that it stretches the limits
Of the date, pushes them back, breaks them? But what, I per-
    sisted,
Have you produced out of your hats, what reasons
Have you for laughing, when I can see you still
Sweating over your labor and see you at evening
Wearily mug up your books. Your eyelids are black, your nights
Are too short for you, much, the drudgery of your days
The threat of death: have you forgotten them laughing?
Then it seemed to me that the laughter came not from those
    people's throats
As though their existence were laughter, as though not one of them
    could
Stop if he tried. I burst myself laughing.

Lied vom Biermann

Wo wäre das bier ohne biermann?
Im fass

    Helles bier dunkles bier
    ausgeschenkt nach dort und hier
    Ihr wolltet nicht trinken

Wer trinkt nun das bier dieses biermann?
Der Grass

    Starkes bier dünnes bier
    ausgeschenkt nach dort und hier
    Ihr wolltet nicht trinken

Biermann sei ihrmann?
Achwas!

    Mann ist mann bier ist bier
    Biermann kam von dort nach hier
    Ihr wolltet nicht trinken

Wolf Biermann
(b. 1936)

Song: The Biermann Cometh

Where would beer be without a Biermann?
Not with us

    Pale beer dark beer
    poured out there and here
    you did not want to drink

Who, then, does drink the beer of this Biermann?
Why, Grass

    Strong beer thin beer
    poured out there and here
    you did not want to drink

Biermann is their man?
What pus!

    A man's a man beer is beer
    Biermann came from there to here
    You did not want to drink

Reiner Kunze

ACH FREUND, GEHT ES NICHT AUCH DIR SO?
ich kann nur lieben
        was ich die Freiheit habe
                auch zu verlassen:

dieses Land
diese Stadt
diese Frau
dieses Leben

Eben darum lieben ja
wenige ein Land
manche eine Stadt
viele eine Frau
aber alle das Leben.

Tischrede des Dichters im zweiten mageren Jahr

Ihr, die ihr noch nicht ersoffen seid, Genossen
Im Schmalztopf der privilegierten Kaste
Ach, wie lang schon lag ich euch nicht in den Ohren!

Wenn durch den nächtlichen Fernsehhimmel
Die obligaten Kastraten in eure Kanäle schiffen
Wenn auf euren erblindeten Bildschirmen
Die keimfreien Jungfrauen flimmern
Wenn die Sandmännchen vom Dienst durch die Röhre
Die euch verordneten Schlaftabletten reichen
Das alles noch mag hingehn, Genossen, aber:

Wenn sie euch abfüttern mit ihren verfluchten
Ideologischen Wassersuppen, die feisten Köche
Dann quält mich doch, ich gebe es zu, Heisshunger
Nach eurem Hunger, Genossen, auf schärfere Sachen:
Stück Fleisch in die Zähne. Wollet euch erinnern:
Fast fettlos gebraten, das Salz erst zuletzt dran

OH, FRIEND, DON'T YOU FIND IT'S THE SAME WITH YOU?
I can only love
        what I am also free
                to leave:

this country
this city
this woman
this life

And that's the reason why
so few love a country
some love a city
many love a woman
but all love life

After-dinner Speech of the Poet in the Second Lean Year

You that have not yet gone under, comrades,
In the lard pot of the privileged caste
Oh, how long it's been since I last made demands on your ears!

When through the nightly television sky
The obligatory castrati board your channels
When on your screens gone blind
The germ-free virgins flicker
When the little sandmen of the service hand you
The sleeping tablets prescribed for you through the tube
Comrades, O.K., let it pass, but:

When they force-feed you with their damnable
Ideological water soups, those fat cooks
Then, I admit, I'm tormented by ravenous hunger
For your hunger, comrades, for less insipid fare:
Chunk of meat between one's teeth. Just try to remember:
Fried almost without fat, salt added only at the end

Damit nicht auslaufen die himmlischen Säfte
Dazu mein Salat mit gehörigen Mengen an
Cayenne-Pfeffer, der lang nach dem Essen
Den Gaumen noch foltert, Zitrone und Knoblauch
Im Dampf des Olivöls schwimmen geschlachtet
Die roten Tomaten Arm in Arm mit den Gurken
Zur Hochzeit in knackigen Kähnen des grünen Salats
Und Salz und Salz! Die Weisheit gestorbener Meere:
Das wohlschmeckende, das ungesunde Salz!
Und! Wie wir dann lässig die Milch in uns schütten
Die sanfte, die gute aus bauchigen Bechern!
Da könnt ihr was lernen, ihr Arschlöcher!

O wollet, Freunde, euch bitte erinnern:
Es munden dem Volke die fetten Ochsen
Seit je in der *Pfanne*!
Nicht aber im *Amte*!

Unter uns gesagt: Startet denn wirklich unser nächstes
Grösseres Fressgelage, Genossen
Erst beim Leichenschmaus?!
Am Grabe der Revolution?!

Frage und Antwort und Frage

Es heisst: Man kann nicht mitten im Fluss
die Pferde wechseln
Gut. Aber die alten sind schon ertrunken

Du sagst: Das Eingeständnis unserer Fehler
nütze dem Feind
Gut. Aber wem nützt unsere Lüge?

Manche sagen: Auf die Dauer ist der Sozialismus
gar nicht vermeidbar
Gut. Aber wer setzt ihn durch?

So that the heavenly juices don't run away
Together with it my salad with the proper amount of
Cayenne pepper, which long after the meal
Still stings the palate, lemon and garlic
Slaughtered float in the olive oil's vapor
The red tomatoes arms linked with the cucumbers
For their wedding in crackly boats of green lettuce
And salt and salt! The wisdom of seas that have died:
That delicious, unhealthy condiment, salt!
Later, how coolly we fill ourselves up with milk,
The gentle, wholesome drink from round-bellied beakers!
That should teach you something, you shitbags!

O comrades, please try to remember:
The people have always enjoyed
Fat oxen in their *frying-pans*!
But not in *offices*!

Between ourselves: does our next bigger guzzling session,
Comrades, really not begin
             Till the funeral feast?!
             At the grave of the revolution?!

Question and Answer and Question

They say: You cannot change horses
in midstream.
Right. But the old ones have drowned already.

You say: The admission of our errors
helps the enemy.
Right. But whom do our lies help?

Some say: In the long run socialism
is simply inevitable.
Right. But who will bring it about?

Der Herbst hat seinen Herbst
Sanft
frisst der Schnee die Gärten
Von Buchen blättert der Rost
Und der Wind
mühelos erntet er
Spatzen vom kahlen Gesträuch

Der Herbst hat seinen Herbst
Bald
blüht schon der Winter
Eins nach dem andern
Es betet ihren Rosenkranz
und gelassen die Natur

Wir aber
Ja, aber wir

Bilanzballade im dreissigsten Jahr

Nun bin ich dreissig Jahre alt
Und ohne Lebensunterhalt
Und hab an Lehrgeld schwer bezahlt
Und Federn viel gelassen
Frühzeitig hat man mich geehrt
Nachttöpfe auf mir ausgeleert
Die Dornenkrone mir verehrt
Ich hab sie liegen lassen
    Und doch: Die Hundeblume blüht
    Auch in der Regenpfütze
    Noch lachen wir
    Noch machen wir nur Witze

Warum hat mich mein Vater bloss
Mit diesem folgenschweren Stoss
Gepflanzt in meiner Mutter Schoss
—Vielleicht, damit ich später
Der deutschen Bürokratensau
Balladen vor den Rüssel hau

Autumn Has Its Autumn
Gently
snow eats up the gardens
Rust flakes from the beech trees
And the wind
effortlessly harvests
sparrows from bare shrubs

Autumn has its autumn
Soon
now winter will blossom
One after another
And nonchalantly nature
tells her rosary

But we
Oh, but we

Stock-taking Ballad in the Thirtieth Year

Into my thirtieth year I've turned
With no living to be earned
Paying dear for all I've learned
With many a feather flying
Early honor was my lot
More than one emptied chamber pot
And the crown of thorns I got
I simply left them lying
        And yet: the dog's-tongue flower blooms
        Even in puddles and muck
        We're laughing still
        Still we do nothing but joke

Why only with that fateful thrust
Did my father do it, must
He plant me in my mother's womb
—It could be so that later
With my ballads I could whack
On her snout and on her back

Auf rosarote Pfoten hau
Die fetten Landesväter
Und doch: Die Hundeblume blüht . . .

Ich hab mich also eingemischt
In Politik, das nützte nischt
Sie haben mich vom Tisch gewischt
Wie eine Mücke
Und als ich sie in' Finger stach
Und mir dabei den Stachel brach
Zerrieben sie mich ganz gemach
In kleine Stücke
Und doch: Die Hundeblume blüht . . .

Dies Deutschland ist ein Rattennest
Mein Freund, wenn du dich kaufen lässt
Egal, für Ostgeld oder West
Du wirst gefressen
Und während man noch an dir kaut
Dich schlecht bezahlt und gut verdaut
Bevor der nächste Morgen graut
Bist du vergessen
Und doch: Die Hundeblume blüht . . .

Ich segelte mit steifem Mast
Zu mancher Schönen, machte Rast
Und hab die andern dann verpasst
Es gibt zu viele
Jetzt hat mein schönes Boot ein Leck
Die Planken faulen langsam weg
Es tummeln sich, ich seh mit Schreck
Die Haie unterm Kiele
Und doch: Die Hundeblume blüht . . .

Die Zeit hat ungeheuren Schwung
Paar Jahre bist du stark und jung
Dann sackst du langsam auf den Grund
Der Weltgeschichte
So manche Generation
Lief Sturm auf der Despoten Thron

The German bureaucratic sow
Every fat pink operator
    And yet: the dog's-tongue flower blooms . . .

In other words, I chose to mix
Quite uselessly, in politics
They swept me off with just two flicks
As they would a bee
And when I turned against the hand
That feeds, I broke my sting there and
They grabbed and ground me fine as sand
Religiously
    And yet: the dog's-tongue flower blooms . . .

This Germany is a rat-filled nest
My friend, if hired you do your best
For D-marks, whether east or west
You will be eaten
And while they're nibbling at you still
Paying you badly, digesting well,
Before next morning without fail
You'll be forgotten
    And yet: the dog's-tongue flower blooms . . .

I used to sail with a stiff mast
To many a fair one, where moored fast
I missed the others as they passed
You can't be everywhere
But now my fine boat has a leak
The planks are rotting week by week
And to my horror as I speak
Sharks gather there.
    And yet: the dog's-tongue flower blooms . . .

Time truly hustles us along
A few years you are young and strong
Then slowly down you go among
The dregs of history
We're not the first to fight alone
Trying to smash a despot's throne

Und wurd beschissen um den Lohn
Und ward zunichte

Und doch: Die Freiheitsblume blüht
Auch in der Regenpfütze
Noch lachen wir
Noch machen wir nur Witze

Und doch: Die Hundeblume blüht
Auch in der Regenpfütze
Noch lachen wir.

Gesang für meine Genossen

Jetzt singe ich für meine Genossen alle
das Lied von der verratenen Revolution
für meine verratenen Genossen singe ich
und ich singe für meine Genossen Verräter
Das grosse Lied vom Verrat singe ich
und das grössre Lied von der Revolution
Und meine Gitarre stöhnt vor Scham
und meine Gitarre jauchzt vor Glück
und meine ungläubigen Lippen beten voller Inbrunst
zu MENSCH, dem Gott all meiner Gläubigkeit

Ich singe für meinen Genossen Dagobert Biermann
der ein Rauch ward aus den Schornsteinen
der von Auschwitz stinkend auferstand
in die viel wechselnden Himmel dieser Erde
und dessen Asche ewig verstreut ist
über alle Meere und unter alle Völker
und der jeglichen Tag neu gemordet wird
und der jeglichen Tag neu aufersteht im Kampf
und der auferstanden ist mit seinen Genossen
in meinem rauchigen Gesang

Und ich singe für Eldridge Cleaver
Genosse im Beton-Dschungel von San Francisco
wie er den Schwarzen schwarz auf weiss macht

And get no thanks, not one bare bone
And cease to be.

   And yet: the flower of freedom blooms
   Even in puddles and muck
   We're laughing still
   Still we do nothing but joke

      And yet: the dog's-tongue flower blooms
      Even in puddles and muck
      Still we ~~do nothing but joke~~
          are laughing

Song for my Comrades

For all my comrades now I sing
the song of revolution betrayed
for my betrayed comrades I sing
and sing for my comrades the betrayers
The great song of betrayal I sing
and the greater song of revolution
And my guitar groans with shame
and my guitar whoops with joy
and my unbelieving lips pray devoutly
to MAN, the god of all my believing

I sing for my comrade Dagobert Biermann
who became a wisp of smoke from the chimneys
who rose up stinking from Auschwitz
into the changeable skies of this earth
and whose ashes are scattered for ever
over all the oceans and among all the peoples
and who is murdered anew each day
and who rises again each day in the fight
and who has risen up with his comrades
in my smoky song

And I sing for Eldridge Cleaver
comrade in the concrete jungle of San Francisco
as in black and white he shows the blacks

dass der Feind nicht schwarz ist oder weiss, sondern
schwarz u n d weiss, das singe ich euch
wenn Eldridge seinen monumentalen Niggerarsch
über Washington auf das Weisse Haus pflanzt
Und wie die BLACK PANTHERS ausbrachen aus der Manege,
aus dem bürgerlichen Zirkus, Panik im Publikum
ich singe die Schweine, wie sie aus den Logen fliehn

Und ein Abgesang auf den Genossen Dubček
der jetzt auf dem türkischen Hund ist
und der lieber hätte gehen sollen
den geraden Weg unter das Hackbeil
oder den krummen Weg unter die Panzer
oder hätte schwimmen sollen in seinem Volk
wie der berühmte Fisch des Genossen Mao
Und darum singe ich den heilsamen Hochmut
des Niedergeworfenen gegen alle Reaktion
gegen die Konterrevolution vom 21. August

Ich schreie und schrei die Prosa von Viet-Nam
ich singe die Heuchelei, das exotische Mitleid
den politischen Schwulst von Frieden und Freiheit
Ich singe den schütteren Bart von Onkel Ho,
dem erspart blieb, diesen Krieg zu überleben
den er längst gewonnen hatte, diesen Krieg
der weitertobt in der Zelle von Muhamad Ali
und der täglich verhöhnt wird im Spenden-Rummel
in der behördlich verordneten Solidarität
im Ablasshandel mit den revolutionären Sünden

Und ich singe noch immer auch meine Liebe
zu meiner nacht-nächtlichen Jungfrau
zu meiner heiligen Genossin
die mich in die Schlacht führt und rettet
in der höheren Gerechtigkeit ihres Lächelns
die mir noch immer auch alle Wunden sanft
aus der Stirne küsste, die ich ihr schlug
ja, ich singe den Klassenkampf der Geschlechter
die Befreiung aus dem patriarchalischen Clinch
aus der Leibeigenschaft unserer Leiber

that the enemy is not black or white but
black a n d white, that's what I sing for you
when Eldridge plants his monumental nigger arse
above Washington in the White House
And how the BLACK PANTHERS broke out of the ring,
out of the bourgeois circus, panic in the crowd
I sing of the pigs, how they flee from their boxes

And an envoi for Comrade Dubček
who has gone down the Turkish drain
and who rather should have gone
the straight way under the axe
or the crooked way under the tanks
or should have swum in his people
like the famous fish of Comrade Mao
And that's why I sing of the healthy uppishness
of those cast down in the face of all reaction
in the face of the counter-revolution of August 21st.

And I cry and cry out the prose of Vietnam
I sing of hypocrisy, of exotic compassion
of political bombast about freedom and peace
I sing of the thin beard of Uncle Ho
who was spared from surviving this war
which he'd won long ago, this war
that rages on in the cell of Muhammad Ali
and that's mocked every day in our collection racket
in our official decrees of solidarity
in our indulgences trade in revolutionary sins

And I still sing of my love too
for my night-nightly virgin
for my holy girl comrade
who leads me into battle and saves me
by the higher justice of her smile
who always until now has gently
kissed from my brow every wound that I gave her
Yes, I sing of the class war of the sexes
liberation from the patriarchal clinch
from the bodily possession of our bodies

Und ich singe all meine Verwirrung
und alle Bitternis zwischen den Schlachten
und ich verschweige dir nicht mein Schweigen
—ach, in wortreichen Nächten, wie oft verschwieg ich
meine jüdische Angst, von der ich behaupte
dass ich sie habe—und von der ich fürchte
dass einst sie mich haben wird, diese Angst
Und ich singe laut in den dunklen Menschenwald
und schlag mir den Takt mit meinen Knochen
auf den singenden Bauch der Gitarre

Ich singe den Frieden mitten im Krieg
Aber ich singe auch Krieg in diesem
dreimal verfluchten möderischen Frieden
der ein Frieden ist vom Friedhoffrieden
der ein Frieden ist hinter Drahtverhau
der ein Frieden ist unter dem Knüppel
Und darum singe ich den revolutionären Krieg
für meine dreimal verratenen Genossen
und noch auch für meine Genossen Verräter:
In ungebrochener Demut singe ich den AUFRUHR

Kleiner Frieden

Kinder, die aufwachen
Frauen, die Morgenwäsche machen
Männer, die ein Gedicht schreiben ü b e r :

Kinder
            die aufwachen

Frauen
            die Morgenwäsche machen

Männer
            die ein Gedicht schreiben

And I sing of all my confusion
and of all the bitterness between battles
and I do not keep silent about my silence
—oh, in nights full of words how often
I kept silent about my Jewish fear which I claim
to have—and about which I fear
that one day it will have me, this fear—
And I sing out loud into the dark human forest
and beat out the rhythm with my bones
on the singing belly of my guitar

I sing of peace in the midst of war
But I sing too of war in this
three times accursed and murderous peace
that's a piece of the peace of graveyards
that's a peace behind barbed wire
that's a peace under a truncheon
And that's why I sing of revolutionary war
for my three times betrayed comrades
and even for my comrades the betrayers:
In unbroken humility I sing of REVOLT

Little Peace

Children who wake up
Women who wash clothes in the morning
Men who write poems a b o u t:

Children
        who wake up

Women
        who wash clothes in the morning

Men
        who write poems

Nachricht

Noch findet er statt
der Sonnenaufgang
Die dunkle Nacht, noch
wird sie veranstaltet

Erstaunlich! Auch diese Früh fand ich mich wieder
am Leben. Erleichtert auch merkte ich auf den Atem
dicht neben mir: die Erde ist also noch immer bevölkert

Den Radiomeldungen über die neuesten Fortschritte
der kleineren Kriege kann ich beruhigt entnehmen:
Noch dauert an die Existenz der Gattung Mensch

Ausgerottet, lese ich in der Abendzeitung
hat sich heute noch nicht, was da alltäglich
nach Frieden schreit

Noch findet er statt
der Sonnenaufgang
Die dunkle Nacht, noch
wird sie veranstaltet

News Item

Still it is taking place
the sunrise
The dark night, still
it is being performed

Astonishing! Early this morning too I found myself
Alive. And relieved I grew aware of the breath
close to me: so the earth is inhabited, still

From the radio reports on the latest progress
of minor wars reassured I can gather:
The species Man has not ceased to exist

Not today, I read in the evening paper
have they exterminated themselves, those who daily
cry out for peace

Still it is taking place
the sunrise
The dark night, still
it is being performed

Kurt Bartsch
(b. 1937)

der bunker

manchmal wohnen noch liebespaare in ihm.
in seinen schiessscharten wohnen spatzen.
langsam zerfällt er; davor hat er grosse angst.
er weiss nicht, dass der krieg lange aus ist.

luftschutzkeller

erinnerung, wo nun das brennholz,
auch spinnen auf der lauer liegen:
wir flüchteten, liessen das schweigen,
in jedem winkel liessen wir die angst zurück.

lange danach, als wir schon wieder
um eingewecktes in die keller stiegen,
vermieden wir die kinder anzusehen,
aus furcht, sie könnten unser schweigen deuten.

möbliertes zimmer

als ich eines abends,
zurückkehrend von einer reise,
die wohnungstür aufschloss,
erkannten mich meine stühle nicht mehr.

ohne aussicht, dem tisch näher zu kommen,
zog ich mich in meinen mantel zurück
und ging, ohne gewohnt zu haben.
ich liess meine stühle sitzen.

the pillbox

at times lovers live in it even now.
sparrows live in its loopholes.
slowly it crumbles; that is its great fear.
it doesn't know that the war ended long ago.

air raid shelter

memory, where the firewood is now,
and spiders too lie in wait:
we fled, leaving silence behind,
in every corner we left our terror.

long after, when we had started
going down again to the cellar for bottled fruit,
we avoided looking at the children
for fear they might understand our silence.

furnished room

one evening when, returning
from a journey, I unlocked
the apartment door
my chairs no longer recognized me.

with no hope of getting close to the table
I withdrew into my overcoat
and left without having lived there.
I jilted my chairs.

poesie

die männer im elektrizitätswerk
zünden sich die morgenzigarette an.
sie haben, während ich nachtsüber schrieb,
schwitzend meine arbeitslampe gefüttert.
sie schippten kohlen für ein mondgedicht.

frühstück

unsere kaffeekanne zerbrach.
unfähig, ihren inhalt für sich zu behalten,
teilte sie ihn der tischdecke mit.

meine hand und ich, wir erschraken.
aber mein sohn, während er milch trank,
lachte und war zufrieden mit mir.

poetry

the men at the power station
light their morning cigarettes.
while I was writing at night
sweating they fed my work lamp.
they shovelled coal for a moon poem.

breakfast

our coffeepot broke.
unable to keep its contents to itself
it communicated them to the tablecloth.

my hand and I were startled.
but my son, drinking his milk,
laughed and was pleased with me.

Volker Braun
(b. 1939)

Waldwohnung

Die Uferschenkel halten den Fluss, still liegt er
Der Himmel zieht den Tag unter sein Himbeermaul
Und schluckt ihn langsam, nur der laue Wind
Bleibt zwischen den Lippen aufrecht, dunkel, heiss, fett
Vom Julimahl. Die Disteln warten steif im Gras, warten
Krachend, warten. Die Hänge halmen, prall
Füllt sich das Moos, komm schnell:
                         auch ohne uns
Scheppert die Bahn nachhaus! Die Betten stehen gut
Weiss, sauber, keusch an steilen Wänden ohne uns! Wir hängen
     weit
Jetzt aus der Stadt heraus und über ihre grüne Haut gebeugt:
Die Sonne ist schon unter uns, wir sind nun,
                         du und ich
Wie über uns das Gras: wild, sanft und wie ein Baum
Wehrlos, stark, nackt, von Wolken und von Sand bewohnt
Und wie der Menschheit Anfang: ernst und sorglos, wie die
     Stadt: voll Lärm—
Hier, diesen Pfad, den ich für uns erst öffne: niemand
Sonst weiss von ihm schon: geh ihn bis der Wald
Uns eine Wohnung hergibt, eine Bank, der Baumstumpf ist
Der Tisch, der rote Dornenzweig biegt sich als Tor
Über das letzte Gemach, der Himmel wird
Dicht, fest, keiner zerschmeisst uns dieses Dach, und warm—
Komm schnell:
                das Tier mit den zwei Rücken liegt
An Erd und Himmel eingestemmt, vier Beine streckts
Vier Arme schlingts um sich und schützt sich selbst vor sich
Und greift sich an und quält sich, und der Haut der Stadt
Bringts Zärtlichkeit bei
                         Und morgen kehrn wir heim
In Bahn und Stadt und Wände: Wald und Gras in uns
In dem Gestein schnell, im Lärm sanft, die Lippen sind
Dann schön.

A Place in the Wood

The thighs of the banks hold the river in, quiet it lies
The sky draws the day up to its raspberry mouth
And slowly gulps it down, only the tepid wind
Remains upright between those lips, dark, hot and greasy
From the July meal. The thistles wait stiffly amid the grass, wait
Cracking, wait. The slopes are blady, round
And full swells the moss, come quickly:
                                        without us too
The train will rattle home! There the beds are, nice and
White, clean, chaste against sheer walls without us. Now
We hang far out of town, bent over its green skin:
The sun's below us, now we
                        you and I
Are like the grass above us: wild, gentle and like a tree
Defenceless, strong, naked, inhabited by clouds and by sand
And like man's beginning: serious and carefree, like the town:
    full of noise—
Look, this path, which I open for us: no one
Else knows of it yet: walk it till the wood
Yields us a dwelling, a bench, that tree stump is
Our table, that twig of red thorns curves as a doorway
Over the last bedroom, the sky grows
Waterproof, solid, no one will smash this roof of ours, and warm—
Come quickly:
                the beast with two backs lies
Wedged between earth and sky, it extends four legs
Winds four arms around itself and protects itself from itself
And attacks itself and torments itself, and teaches the skin
    of the town
How to be tender.
                        And we shall go home tomorrow
To train and town and walls: wood and grass inside us
Among the stonework quick, among the noise gentle, then our
    lips will
Be beautiful.

Provokation für A. P.

1
Alle Sekunden der Freude
Die Stunden des Taus und der müden Sonne
Das Wandern die Lenden der Wiesenberge hinab
Das Liegen in den fetten Armen einer hergelaufenen Nacht
Das Schweigen vor den Motoren und Fliederbäumen
All das Besinnen, Behalten, Dableiben
Alles Besinnen will ich fortgeben, ausspeien, auslöschen
Fliesst aus mir fort mit den Ergüssen des Frühlings

Ich melde meinen Verzicht an auf den Abend und auf die Nacht.

2
Ich bin der selbstloseste nicht unter deinen Verehrern.
Ich liebe den Tag, wenn er dann auf die Dächer springt.
Und ich liebe die Hilflosigkeit deines Mundes
Ich liebe die ganze Zuversicht deiner Arme.

3
Ich will nicht ausruhn bei dir, Freundin
Ich habe keine Geduld für deine Lust
Ich bin zu unbescheiden, dich zu lieben
Du sollst dich dem Tag geben vor unserer Nacht
Dein Leib, Bett oder Sarg unserer Kinder
Deine Schenkel, helle Stützen der Traumgewölbe
Deine Brauen, Flügel der Augen
Sind mir so fern und nah
Wie der endliche Tag, dem du gehörst.

4
Der Ungeduldige bin ich unter den Ungeduldigsten
Veränderlich bin ich in den Veränderungen.

Und ich weiss: ich bin deine Liebe wert
Und ich weiss: du bringst sie mir selbst entgegen
Wenn du veränderlich bist mit deinem Land
Und keinen Schritt breit nehm ich dir ab.

Provocation for A.P.

1
All the seconds of joy
The hours of dew and of the tired sun
Wading down the loins of the meadow hills
Lying in the fat arms of a stray night
Being silent in front of motors and lilac trees
All our thinking things over, retaining, remaining
All thinking I'll give away, spew out, extinguish
They flow out of me together with spring's effusions

I report my renunciation of evening and of night

2
I am not the most unselfish of your admirers.
I love day, if it then jumps on to the roofs.
And I love the helplessness of your mouth
I love all the confidence of your arms.

3
It is not rest that I want of you, girl
I have no patience for your pleasure
I'm too immodest to love you
You should give yourself to day before our night
Your body, bed or coffin for our children
Your thighs, bright pillars of dream vaults
Your eyebrows, wings of the eyes
Are as far and near to me
As the finite day to which you belong

4
I'm the impatient one among the most impatient
Changeable I am among the changes

And I know: I'm worthy of your love
And I know: you offer it to me yourself
If you're changeable as your country changes
And I will not save you the length of a single pace.

Vorläufiges

Andere werden kommen und sagen: EHRLICH waren sie
(Das ist doch schon was zuzeiten der Zäune und Türschlösser)
Sie schrieben für das Honorar und die Befreiung der Menschheit
Einst, als die Verse noch Prosa warn (wenig Dichter, viel Arbeit)—
Aber was für Klötze! Wie hieben sie Menschen zurecht:

Mit Schraubenschlüsseln wollten sie Brustkästen öffnen,
    Quälerei!
Make-up mit dem Vorschlaghammer! Liebesgeflüster auf
    Kälberdeutsch!
Revolution mit der Landsknechttrommel—wussten sie nichts von
    Lippen
Die unmerklich beben beim Abprall der neuen Worte?
Mussten sie neue Ufer zertosen mit ihrem Wortsturm?

Ach, ihr seid besser dran: eurer blosses Ohr wird Herztöne
    auffangen
Eure blossen Worte werden wie Verse schon Zäune umlegen
Eure Revolution wird vielleicht ein Gesellschaftsspiel, heiter,
    planvoll.
Dann werden unsere Wiesen nur Grashalme sein
Und was uns Sturm ist, ist euch nur lauer Wind.

Doch wir nehmen es auf uns: vergessen zu sein am Mittag!
Denn auch ihr werdet das Feuer der Revolution in euch tragen
    und den Wind Widerspruch:
Dass das Feuer zur Flamme aufsprüh, bedarf es des Windes.
Und auch ihr werdet für die Befreiung der Menschheit schreiben
    und für ihre Qual:
Weil sie nur vorläufig ist, werdet ihr Vorläufige sein.

Temporary

Others will come and say: they were HONEST
(And that is something in times of padlocks and fences),
They wrote for a fee and the greater freedom of men,
In those days, when verse was still prose (much work and few
    poets)—
But what clods! How they beat people into shape:

Tormented them, trying to unlock heartchambers with wrenches!
Make-up put on with sledgehammers! Wooing by giggly bumpkins!
Revolution with banners and drums—did they know nothing of
    lips
That tremble invisible as new words spring from them?
Did they have to blast new shores with their storms of words?

Ah, you are better at it: your ear alone will register heartbeats,
Your words alone like verse will overturn fences,
Your revolution might well be a party game, merry and well
    planned.
Then our meadows will be just grass stalks,
And what to us is a storm is to you just a mild wind.

We accept, then, to be forgotten at midday.
For you too will carry the fire of revolution within you and the
    worrying wind:
Fire needs the wind to spark into flame.
And you too will write for the freedom of men and for their
    torment:
Which is temporary, as you too will be.

Landgang

1

Wie weit, in den harten Himmel geschlagen
Kanossas, weit
Bin ich fortgelangt aus meinem Land
Auf den täglichen Dienstwegen, eine Behausung
Zum Beispiel oder zwei Sack Zement
Zu erhalten, in den Schalterstunden
Am geheiligten Dienstag. In des Ufers
Unflat, gegen Abend
Lieg ich, das der Fluss bezog
Mit Kot und Laugen, in den Rosenbüschen
Müde im Mantel, den ich mir umwarf
Vor den Vorzimmern der sorgenvollen
Gottheiten, zu denen ich zähle.
Und ich blicke auf mein Land hin
Im frischen Spiegel aus Schlamm
Das erkenn ich nicht.
Im Fluss, der dunkel wird
Schwimmt sehr fern meine Stadt
Ein weisser Wal.

Und ich folgte den ganzen Tag nur
Den Bräuchen der Sozietät: wie weit
Müssen hier alle ausser Landes sein
Gegen Abend! Immer zwischen den Flüssen
Falten sie, im Schlamme, ihre Glieder aus
Watend bei den Rosen. Und sie sehn
Wie auf weisse Wale
Auf ihre Städte hin.

Andere sind weiter fortgelangt als ich
Bis in des Lands andern Teil.
An einem Morgen, nach den Abenden
Hatten sie die Suche nach ihrem Land
Schon aufgegeben.

An einem Morgen, jeden Tag
Seh ich ein Land

In the country

1
How far, beaten into the hard sky
Of Canossa, far
Have I gone out of my country
Along official daily channels, to find
A place to live or two bags of cement
During working hours
On Holy Tuesday. In the filth
Of the bank, towards evening
I lie, which the river has covered
With turds and scum, in the rosebushes
Tired in my coat, which I wrapped round me
Before the antechambers of the anxious
Gods, among whom I am counted.
And I look out across my country
In the fresh mirror of slime
And do not recognize it.
In the darkening river
At a great distance my town is swimming
A white whale.

And I followed the whole day through only
The customs of society: how far
Must everyone here be abroad
Towards evening! Always between the rivers
They unfold their limbs in the slime
Wading by the roses. And they look
As at white whales
Across at their towns.

Others have gone farther than I
Into the country's other part.
One morning, after those evenings
They had given up the search
For their country.

One morning, every day
I see a country

Über dem blanken Fluss
Die Stadt, unbekannt. Das hier
Wer weiss, mag mein Land sein.
Es ist Mittwoch. Nicht sehr zugetan
All den Gegenständen, mitleidlos, geb ich
Was mich berührt dem Fluss. Die Luft
Dröhnt, die Rauchpfeile verfinstern
Den Himmel wieder. Auf dem Asfalt bewegt sich
Industrie auf Industrie zu. Langsam wächst der Beton
Hell um das Eisen zwischen die Bäume ein. Manchmal
Scheint mir ein Weg bekannt. Diesen
Umgeh ich. Als wär alles neu wähl ich
Unter den Landschaften. Fern
Steh ich, nur mit den Sohlen, im Land.

2
Weit vor den Ausfallstrassen
Vor dem verlassenen Land seh ich
Neben mir, am hellen Tag, so weit
Fortgelangt in den schwachen Strassenbahnen
Viele. Und sie gehn
Weiter, wo sich der Boden aufwälzt
Zu seiner Gestaltung, und wo manche auch
Verweilen in den Fahnen, gehn sie
Weiter. Diese etwa
Kenne ich, die wachsen aus diesem Land
Und ziehn es mit an den Sohlen
Weiter.

Aber wie weit
Muss ich, bis zu welchen Schritt, und ihr
Gehn, wieviel, auf den täglichen Dienstwegen
Gebe ich auf! Mit jedem Jahr
Entfern ich mich mehr. Wir aber
Kommen uns näher. Manchmal, schon
In den festeren Ufern seh ich
Die Stadt: das weisse Lid
Für eine Nacht vor dem Auge. Immer leichter
Entkomm ich dem Land. Leichter
Kommt das Land mit uns.

Over the smooth river
The town, unknown. Here
Who knows, my country might be.
It's Wednesday. Caring little
For all these things, pitiless, I give
What moves me to the river. The air
Resounds, smoke arrows darken
The sky again. On asphalt industry
Moves toward industry. Concrete spreads slowly,
Bright around the iron between the trees. Sometimes
A path seems familiar to me. And I
Avoid it. As if everything were new I choose
Between the landscapes. Distant
I stand, with the soles of my feet alone, in the country.

2
The disused roads the abandoned
Country far behind, I can see many people
Near me, in bright daylight, they
Have come so far in rundown
Trams. And they are going
Farther; where the earth heaves
To shape itself, and where some
Stay behind among the flags, they
Go still farther. These people
I know, I think; they grow out of this country
And carry it with them on their soles
Still farther.

But how far
Must I, up to which step, and you
Go, how much, along the official daily channels
Do I give up! With every year
I go farther away. But we
Come closer together. Already within
Firmer banks, I sometimes see
The town: the white lid
For a night over its eye. Ever more easily
I escape the country. More easily
The country comes with us.

Provokation für mich
(*Als im dritten Viertel des* 20. *Jahrhunderts die Gedichte entbehrlich wurden*)

1
Genossen, ausdauernd
Preisen wir das Positive.
Die Postfrau grüsst nicht freundlicher.
Die Mädchen lieben uns und loben uns nicht.
Die Freunde loben uns, aber lieben uns nicht.
Man verweigert uns das Honorar der Herzen.

2
Wir schreiben aber für diese Leute:
Ihre Hände preisen das Positive, jeder Finger
Preist es, die Fingerspitzen, die Fäuste.
Ich bin mit der Postfrau unter die Dächer gestiegen
Ich habe der Freunde Herzen belagert und durchsucht
Ich hab Expeditionen über Mädchenstirnen geschickt
Ich hab in Furchen, die die Sorge gräbt, wachgelegen.
Ich weiss: all diese Leute preisen das Positive.

3
Aber die Postfrau trägt nicht nur Ruhmeskantaten aus.
Die Mädchen lieben nicht, der nichts begehrt.
Die Freunde loben nicht tollkühn wie wir:
Sie preisen den Plan, indem sie ändern.
Wir aber rühmen nur, bessern nichts, sind entbehrlich
Wir nehmen uns selbst nicht für voll.
Uns nenn ich noch: negative Dichter.

Der Ostermarsch

Am Rande der Stadt
Wo die Garagen gedeihn
Im Tale grünet Hoffnungsglück, dort
Draussen dürfen sie gehn, vom Dunst
Der Gärten verhängt, wo Zwerge wachen
Uber den Frieden zum Schein

Provocation for Me
(when in the third quarter of the twentieth century poems became
dispensable)

1
Comrades, persistent
We celebrate what is positive.
The postwoman's "good morning" is no friendlier.
The girls love us and do not praise us.
Our friends praise us but do not love us.
They refuse us the honorarium of hearts.

2
Yet we write for those people:
Their hands celebrate what is positive, every finger
Celebrates it, their fingertips, their fists.
I have joined the postwoman's round, climbing stairs
I have besieged and searched the hearts of my friends
I have despatched expeditions across the foreheads of girls
I have lain awake in furrows ploughed by care.
I know: all these people celebrate what is positive.

3
But the postwoman doesn't deliver only cantatas of thanksgiving.
The girls don't love the man who desires nothing.
Our friends don't praise with our crazy recklessness.
They celebrate the plan by making changes.
But we only praise, don't improve anything, are dispensable.
We don't think ourselves quite responsible.
For the time being I call us negative poets.

The Easter March

On the city's fringe
Where the garages thrive
In the valley a joyous hope grows green, far
Out they're allowed to be, veiled
By vapors from gardens where gnomes watch
Over peace apparently

Eine Bannmeile weg von den Kirchen
Und Plätzen, gedrängt
Aus dem Blick der Bürger
Jeder sonnt sich heute so gern
In den Nebenstrassen, ab-
Gemessenen Schritts, mit gemeldeter Miene
Gehn sie, nach Vorschrift verfolgt
Von Überfallwagen, heran

An den Kern der Stadt
Den nehmen sie in die Zange
Laut und brechen das alte Gehäuse
Auf mit ihrem Tritt: mit Schlaggeigen
Und unfrommen Kutten streichen
Sie grell den Markt und singen
Sich aus dem Schlaf, weissagend
Die schwarze Zeit: bis aus geheimen
Gängen, pfeifend, falln
Die Maden in Monturen
Die Ämter verblühn, reif
Für einen Sturm
Der liegt noch gefangen an vielen
Gaumen, im traurigen Lied, und weicht
Mit dem Zug aus Weichbild der Stadt
Zertrennt von gläsernen Wänden
Hier bleiben die Werte stabil
Zufrieden jauchzet gross und klein
Der Zug ziehen schweigend ab, ab-
Geschlagen von den Strafen
Wo die Bürger auferstehn
Hier ist das Volkes wahrer Himmel
Zu den Ascheplätzen, ungeleitet
An der Stadt vorbei

An den Rand
Wo dies Land ist.

A mile's ban away from the churches
And squares, squeezed
Out of the citizens' vision
Everyone likes to sunbathe today
In the side streets, at a
Measured pace, with permitted expressions
They go, legally pursued
By attackers, toward

The city center
Which with a pincer movement they
Noisily seize, breaking open the old shell
With their footfall; with guitars
And impious cowls they strafe
The marketplace blaringly, singing
Themselves awake, foretelling
The black time; until out of secret
Passages, whistling, the maggots
In uniform fall,
The offices wilt, ripe
For a storm
That still lies captive upon
Many palates, in a sad song, and retreats
With the procession toward the city's retreats
Divided by glass walls
Here values remain stable
Loudly do great and small rejoice
The procession leaves in silence, di-
Rected out of those streets
Where the citizens rise again
Here is the people's veritable heaven
To the garbage disposal plots, diverted
Past the city

To the fringe
Where this country lies.

Schauspiel

Das ist kein Geheimnis mehr:
Wir lassen uns nichts mehr vormachen.
Wir sitzen nicht stur mit glotzenden Augen.
Wir trommeln nicht Beifall auf die Folterbänke.
Wir zahlen nicht gröhlend das Spiel der Grossen
Das Schlachten der Körper oder wenigstens Seelen.
Der Auftritt der Massen hat begonnen
Auf der grell beleuchteten Szene:
Überall finden Proben statt ohne Netz
Auf den Strassen, Kathedern und Partituren.
(Nur das Banjo darf noch nicht spielen.)
Fernrohre sind auf die Ränge montiert
Die Zeichen der Zeit zeitig zu entdecken.
Souffleure funken ratlos dazwischen
Und drehn sich fröhlich das Wort im Mund um.
Jeder sagt was er denkt—wir spielen das Stück
Unsres Lebens. Es kann nicht mehr abgesetzt werden.
(Das Banjo wartet auf seinen Einsatz.)
Verstandlich wie eine Losung, leicht wie ein Gewand
Das jeden passt, führn wir sie langsam herauf:
Die Freiheit.

Prometheus

Weg, blinde Hoffnung, die unsre Städte
Beschlägt, süsser Dunst
Und unsre Felder jaucht
Mit Spülicht aus Kinos und Kneipen:
Was geht denn gut
Wenn wir es nicht versehn, jeder
Wie unsern Herd, auf dem wir
Selber die Suppe kochen?

Ich fliege am Himmel
Nicht nur in Gedanken:

Performance

This is no longer a secret:
We'll not be hoodwinked again.
We don't sit here dumb with gaping eyes.
We don't drum applause on to the torturers' racks.
We don't pay grizzling for the great ones' play
The butchering of bodies or souls at least.
The entrance of the masses has begun
On the glaringly lighted stage:
Everywhere rehearsals take place without a net
In the streets, at the reading desks and scores.
(Only the banjo must not play yet.)
Telescopes are focused on to the rows of seats
To discover the signs of the time in time.
Prompters interrupt with frantic transmissions
And cheerfully turn around the words in their mouths.
Everyone says what he thinks—we act the play
Of our life. It can't be taken off now.
(The banjo waits for its part to begin.)
Understandable as a password, light as a garment
That fits anyone, we slowly lead it in:
Freedom.

Prometheus

Away, blind hope that mists over
Our cities, sweet vapor
And manures our fields
With swill from cinemas, bars:
What does go well
If we don't look after it, each one of us,
As we do our stoves on which
We cook our own soup?

I hover in the sky
Not only in my thoughts:

Was uns Neues gelingt, sprengt
Fast die Adern vor Schmerz, und dröhnt
Die zuschaun, in den Ohren. Noch die Luft
Müssen wir uns erzeugen
Im leeren Raum.

Ich seh die Länder, gezeichnet
Von einem Schein, den sie wahren
Wie lange? Drohnd machen alte
Landstriche, quer
Durch die Welt, ihre letzten
Versuche, mit unbeherrschter
Kraft. Die Flugzeuge gehn durch die schwachen
Lappen des Himmels
Und das gelegt wird, unser Feuer
Löscht uns aus.

Und im friedlichen Land:
Liegt die Zukunft da, leicht
Wie auf der Zunge? die Erde
Bricht sich wie Brot an den Lippen
Das Leben fällt in den Schoss
Zu unsern Händen? die Bücher
Leben? Woher denn
Woher auf andre Art
So grosse Hoffnung?

Kein Haus steht
Wenn Wir es nicht erhalten
Das Land, bei leichtem Regen
Sackt weg. Wo wir nicht sind
Und sehn, geht etwas vor
Das wir nur ahnen
Das schiesst ins Kraut und nicht nur
Und wie Hoffnung, das zieht auf mich her
Ein trübes verlorenes Wetter—

Was glaub ich denn
Wenn nicht an uns? worauf
Hoffe ich sonst: ist unsre Hand

The new thing that we achieve
Nearly bursts our veins with anguish and roars
In the ears of those who look on. The very air
We have to create for ourselves
In empty space.

I saw the countries marked
By a radiance which they fend off.
How long? Threatening, old regions
Diagonally across
The world, make their last
Attempts, with uncontrolled
Power. The aeroplanes fly through the feeble
Rags of the sky
And that which is laid, our fire
Extinguishes us.

And in the peaceful country:
Does the future lie there, light
As upon the tongue? the earth
Break like bread on the lips
Life drop on our laps
Together with our hands? Do the books
Live? Then from where
From where in a different way
Such a great hope?

No house stands up
If we do not maintain it
The land, in light rain
Erodes. Where we are not
Nor look, something is happening
Which we only guess
This proliferates and not only this
And like hope, this draws closer to me
A dull lost weather—

What do I believe
If not in us? for what
Else do I hope; are our hands

Faul, unser Feuer? Was
Schlag ich die Augen nieder
Vor den Schlägen der Zeit: ist hier
Nichts m e h r zu machen? das
Nimmt uns keiner ab; wolln wir
In Vorzimmern warten auf
Die neue Verfügung?

Auf diese Zeit nicht, auf nichts
Vertrauend als auf uns, nicht
Mit freudig geschlossenen Augen;
Bedroht, aber nicht gedrillt
Sieht mich der Tag
Der widerstrahlt
Wenn wir unser Feuer tragen
In den Himmel.

Fragen eines Arbeiters während der Revolution

So viele Berichte.
So wenig Fragen.
Die Zeitungen melden unsere Macht.
Wie viele von uns
Nur weil sie nichts zu melden hatten
Halten noch immer den Mund versteckt
Wie ein Schamteil?
Die Sender funken der Welt unsern Kurs.
Wie, an den laufenden Maschinen, bleibt
Uns eine Wahl zwischen zwei Hebeln?—
Auf den Plätzen stehn unsere Namen.
Steht jeder auf dem Platz
Die neuen Beschlüsse
Zu verfügen? Manche verfügen sich nur
In die Fabriken. Auf den Thronen sitzen
Unsre Leute: fragt ihr uns
Oft genug? Warum
Reden wir nicht immer?

Lazy, our fire? Why
Do I lower my glance
Under the blows of the age: is there
Nothing m o r e to be done here? No one
Will swallow that; are we
To wait in anterooms for
The new dispensation?

Not in this age, trusting
In nothing but ourselves, not
With happily closed eyes;
Threatened but not drilled
The day will see me
That, radiant, reflects
When we carry our fire
Up to the sky.

Questions of a Worker during the Revolution

So many news items.
So few questions.
The newspapers report that we are in power.
How many of us
Only because we had nothing to report
Even now keep our mouths hidden
Like private parts?
The transmitters broadcast our course to the world.
How, at the running machines, does
A choice remain for us between two levers?—
At our places you'll read our names.
Does each of us occupy
The place where the new resolutions
Are drafted? Some only draft
Themselves into factories. On the thrones our
People sit: do you ask us
Often enough? Why
Don't we speak all the time?

Bernd Jentzsch
(b. 1940)

Die grünen Bäume starben in uns ab

Die grünen Bäume mit den schwarzen Stämmen
wuchsen in uns ein und starben in uns ab.

Die Elemente der Erde, Phosphor und Schwefel,
fielen aus den Wolken am Tag und in der Nacht.

Sirenen sägten Bunker in den Schlaf,
ein Taschenlampenstrahl war der Abendstern.

Die Mäntel trugen wir übereinander.
Blicke glitten nach oben, wo auch Stare flogen.

Die roten Städte mit den schwarzen Haaren
glichen nicht den Städten aus dem Bilderbuch.

Die wir unsere Väter nannten, erklärten nichts.
Ihre Stimmen schwiegen unter Befehlen und Schnee.

In den Wäldern toter Strassen und im Geäst
des Vogelflugs erwachten wir zu plötzlich.

Die uns hätten Gefährten werden können,
trugen keine Haut auf dem Gesicht.

Wir suchen nach der Haut unserer Gefährten
in den Gesichtern derer, die noch leben.

Zorn wohnt in uns und Hoffnung ist da,
wenn wir an grüne Bäume denken.

Meine Mutter

1
Im Bündel drei Nesselhemden, so ging sie
Los, das war alles, vom Land
In die sächsische Hauptstadt, ein

The Green Trees Died Within Us

The green trees with the black trunks
grew into us and in us died away.

Earth's elements, phosphor and brimstone,
fell out of the clouds by day and in the night.

Sirens sawed bunkers into our sleep,
a flashlamp beam became the evening star.

The overcoats we wore layer on layer.
Our gaze slid upward, where starlings also flew.

The red cities with black hair
were not like the cities in the picture books.

Those whom we called our fathers explained nothing.
Their voices fell silent under commands and snow.

In the forests of dead streets and in the boughs
of birdflight we awoke too suddenly.

Those who might have become our companions
wore no skin on their faces.

We look for the skin of our companions
in the faces of those still living.

Anger's at home in us and hope is there
whenever we remember the green trees.

My Mother

1
In her bundle three muslin shirts, that's how she went
Off, that was all, from the country
To the Saxon capital, a

Mädchen, das höchstens
Von Sprüchen zehrte: Wenn du mir Schande machst,
Schick ich den Strick.

Weissnähen, Schneidern, am Sonntag
Hielt einer um ihre Hand an und pries den
Königin-Luisen-Bund. Ein anderer,
Blendend weiss die Manschetten, pries nur sie,
Der wurde genommen, dann sie,
Ihre Zeit verging beschwerlich, ein Sohn,
Sagte der Arzt, der Mann
Einberufen, Fallschirmjäger,
Überwiegend Kreta, dort blieb er, nun
Ein ganz ruhiger Beamter
Unter dem Himmel und unter der Erde.

2
Im Mai der Frieden, sie führte
Krieg gegen die leeren Teller, gegen
Die Kälte, die Hausierer, den Schlaf,
Mit allen Mitteln, mit Nadel und Faden,
Bis er gross war, der Sohn,
Über den Berg und über alle Berge, jetzt

Wehrt sie sich nicht mehr, gibt nach
Dem eigenen Alter und summt vor sich hin.

Mann zum Jahreswechsel 45/46

Wozu denn zwei Söhne, wofür
Der eine bei Narvik, der andre
Hinter der Wolga, vermisst, und beide,
Wozu denn, verloren, die Wohnung, unser
Bescheidener Laden, wozu denn,
Kurz vorm Ende, eine Sprengbombe
War es, und selbst noch die Frau,
Wozu denn das alles und so unwiderruflich, für wen
Das nackte Leben retten, das Hemd wechseln,
Das Jahr, wozu denn das Glas erheben
Und auf wen.

Girl who subsisted
On mottoes at best: If you dishonor me,
I shall send the rope.

Patching, tailoring, on Sunday
Somebody asked for her hand and praised the
German Conservative Union. Another,
His cuffs a dazzling white, praised only her
And was taken, then she.
Her time passed with difficulties, a son,
Said the doctor, her husband
Conscripted, parachute corps,
Crete above all, there he remained, now
A very quiet official
Under the sky and under the earth.

2
In May the armistice, she waged
War on empty plates, on
The cold, the hawkers, and sleep
With every weapon she had, with needle and thread,
Till he was grown up, the son
Over the hills and over all hills, now

She no longer resists, gives in
To her own old age and hums to herself.

Man at the Turn of the Year 45/46

What for, two sons, then, what for
The one at Narvik, the other
Behind the Volga, reported missing, and both,
What for, then, lost, the apartment, our
Little shop, what for, then,
Just before the end, a high explosive bomb
It was, and the wife too,
What for, all that and so irrevocable, for whose sake
Get away with bare life, change shirts,
Change years, what for, raise the glass
And to whom.

NEW HANOVER COUNTY

831
H

S

Hamburger, Michael
,ed.
East German Poetry.

6/7

Wilmington Public Library
Wilmington, NC 28401